Lost Coast Review
Winter 2016
Volume 7, Number 2

Avignon Press

Cover Image: *The Beauty of Indecisions*, by Ernest Williamson. Reproduced with permission from the artist.

AVIGNON PRESS
Newport Beach, CA, USA
ISBN: 978-0-9962920-9-2
ISSN 2332-4805

Lost Coast Review

Volume 7, Number 2, Winter 2016

Editorial Staff

Editor-in-Chief	Casey Dorman
Associate Editor	Darryl Freeland
Short Story Editor	Diane Rogers
Book Review Editor	Noel Mawer
Film Review Editor	Hadley Hury
Poetry Editor	Randall Mawer
Business/Marketing Mgr.	Lai Le Dorman

Publisher: Avignon Press

LOST COAST REVIEW is published quarterly by AVIGNON PRESS, at 41 Shearwater Place, Newport Beach, CA 92660. Lost Coast Review welcomes unsolicited submissions of short stories, poetry, book and film reviews. Please see submissions page for instructions on submissions. Subscriptions of Lost Coast Review may be purchased for $20/year (plus postage). Subscriptions and individual copies of Lost Coast Review may be purchased through the publisher's website at www.avignonpress.com or by accessing the online version at www.lostcoastreview.com

Contents

Contributors

Charlie Keys Bohem (Essay/Prose Poem: *Orange County Seafood*) is a freshman at Vassar College, where he pretends to be studying chemistry and mostly plays the guitar. He is nineteen years old and at this point chiefly writes stories about nineteen year olds.

Wayne Christeson (Essay: *Raymond Chandler*) a retired attorney, lives on a farm in Leiper's Fork, Tennessee. He is a graduate of Vanderbilt University, and won second prize in the national "Write Like Raymond Chandler" competition sponsored by The Library of America. His work has appeared in *Vanderbilt Magazine*, *Nashville Arts Magazine*, *The Nashville SCENE*, and other publications. He serves as copy-editor for the online book review *Chapter 16*.

J.A. Camrose (Two Poems) is a contemporary poet residing in Minneapolis, Minnesota.

Elizabeth Crowell (Poetry: "No Early Birds") was born and raised in NJ. She received her B.A. from Smith College and her M.F.A. in poetry from Columbia University. Her work has been published recently in *Storm Cellar*, *The Bellevue Literary Review*, *Pea River Review*, and other publications. She lives with her wife and children outside Boston

Darren Demaree (Three Poems) has had poems appear, or are scheduled to appear in numerous magazines/journals, including the *South Dakota Review*, *Meridian*, *The Louisville Review*, *Diagram*, and the *Colorado Review*. He is the author of *As We Refer To Our Bodies* (2013, 8th House), *Temporary Champions* (2014, Main Street Rag), *The Pony Governor* (2015, After the Pause Press), and *Not For Art Nor Prayer* (2015, 8th House). He is the Managing Editor of the *Best of the Net Anthology*. He is currently living and writing in Columbus, Ohio with his wife and children.

Craig Evenson (Poetry: "Owled") has had his poems in various publications, including *The Midwestern Quarterly*, *The Meridian Anthology of*

Contemporary Poetry, Off the Coast, and *Iodine Review*. He has work forthcoming in *Hurricane Review, Fractal Literary Magazine, Inscape* and *Stillwater Review*.

Allen Forrest (Two Cartoons) Graphic artist and painter Allen Forrest was born in Canada and bred in the U.S. He has created cover art and illustrations for literary publications and books. He is the winner of the Leslie Jacoby Honor for Art at San Jose State University's *Reed Magazine* and his Bel Red painting series is part of the Bellevue College Foundation's permanent art collection. Forrest's expressive drawing and painting style is a mix of avant-garde expressionism and post-Impressionist elements reminiscent of van Gogh, creating emotion on canvas.

Joe Giordano (Short Story: *A Matter of Honor*) Joe's stories have appeared in more than seventy magazines including *Bartleby Snopes, The Monarch Review, decomP,* and *Shenandoah*. His novel, *Birds of Passage, An Italian Immigrant Coming of Age Story*, was published by *Harvard Square Editions* October 2015. Read the first chapter and sign up for his blog at http://joe-giordano.com/

Carolyn Gregory (Two Poems) Carolyn Gregory's poems and music essays have been published in *American Poetry Review, Main Street Rag, Off the Coast, Cutthroat, Bellowing Ark, Seattle Review, Big River Review, Tower Journal,* and *Stylus*. She was nominated for a Pushcart Prize and previously won a Massachusetts Cultural Council Award. Her first book, *Open Letters*, was published in 2009 and a second book, *Facing The Music*, was published in Florida in 2015. She is currently working on her third book of poetry. And is also starting to write short stories after many years of only writing poetry.

Cristine A. Gruber (Two Poems) writes from sunny, Southern California. She has had work featured in numerous magazines, including: *North American Review, Writer's Digest, California Quarterly, The Homestead Review, Red River Review, The Tule Review,* and *The Write Place at the Write Time*. Her first full-length collection of poetry, *Lifeline*, is available from http://buybooksontheweb.com. More of Cristine's work can be found and enjoyed at http://sierraviewjournal.blogspot.com/

Nels Hanson (Three Poems) grew up on a small farm in the San Joaquin Valley of California and has worked as a farmer, teacher and contract writer/editor. His fiction received the San Francisco Foundation's James D. Phelan Award and Pushcart nominations in 2010, 12, and 2014. Poems appeared in *Word Riot, Oklahoma Review, Pacific Review* and other magazines and received a 2014 Pushcart nomination, *Sharkpack Review's* 2014 Prospero Prize, and 2015 and 2016 Best of the Net nominations..

Hadley Hury (Film Reviews: *Three for Your Consideration*) has had his poetry and short fiction appear in *Forge Journal, Off the Coast, Appalachian Heritage, The James Dickey Review, Colorado Review, Avatar, Image, Green Mountains Review* and numerous other journals, reviews, and magazines. He has published a novel and a collection of short stories, and was for ten years film critic for The Memphis Flyer. He has also been an associate professor in film at the University of Memphis and lecturer in film at Rhodes College, The Memphis College of Art, and the Brooks Museum. He lives with his wife Marilyn in Louisville, Kentucky. Hadley is the Film Review Editor for *Lost Coast Review*.

John Horvath Jr. (Poetry: "George and his Wife") has published widely since the 1960s in European, Asian, Australian, African, and Middle Eastern magazines as well as American and Canadian Journals. After spending his youth frivolously in the South Chicago area, he spent 13 years in the military and a like number of years as an academic (pre-school care giver to college department chair). Now disabled from a bad parachute jump and retired, he lives with his wife and family, many dogs, and two cats in Mississippi.

Mike James (Poetry: "Side Door Blessing") has had recent poems in Iodine and Comstock Review. New work is forthcoming *in The Chiron Review, Poem,* and *Negative Capability*. He has published seven poetry collections. The two most recent are *Past Due Notices: Poems 1991-2011* (Main Street Rag, 2012) and *Elegy in Reverse* (Aldrich Press, 2014). A new collection, *The Year We Let The House Fall Down*, will be published later this year by Aldrich Press. He livse and work in Douglasville, GA with hiswife and five kids. He also serves as an associate editor at *The Kentucky Review*.

Billie Kelpin (Short Story: *Sylvia*) Billie Kelpin has always been intrigued with language development. This love has led her to a career as a former teacher of the deaf and hard of hearing, sign language interpreter, and creator of online educational learning games for her company, Language Rocks. As a left-handed woman in a right-handed world, Billie has also authored the children's book, *Lucky, the Left-Pawed Puppy* to empower little left-handers. Fascinated with the possibilities of app development for writers, Billie has created the smartphone app, "The Perfect Husband App," and is working on an audio book app, "Live from Milwaukee, It's Tuesday Night," a collection of narrated short stories and essays written by herself and guest authors.

Michael Minassian (Book Review: *The Translator*) lives in San Antonio, Texas. His poems have appeared recently in such journals as *The Broken Plate, Exit 7, Iodine Poetry Journal, Main Street Rag, The Meadow*, and *Visions International*. He is also the writer/producer of the pod cast series Eye On Literature available on I-tunes. Amsterdam Press published his chapbook of poems entitled *The Arboriculturist* in 2010.

Rodney Nelson (Three Poems) lives in the northern Great Plains. His poem "One Winter" won a Poetry Kit Award for 2011 (U.K.); it had appeared in *Symmetry Pebbles*. His "Upstream in Idaho" received a Best of Issue Award at the late *Neon Beam* (also England). He has published the chapbooks *Metacowboy* , *In Wait, Mogollon Picnic, Bog Light, Hill of Better Sleep* and *Sighting the Flood*. The chapbook *Fargo in Winter* took second place in the 2013 Cathlamet Prize competition. *Directions From Enloe* won third in the *Turtle Island Quarterly* contest. His poetry ebook *Nodding in Time* (Kind of a Hurricane Press) will soon be published and the full-length *Felton Prairie* has recently been published by Middle Island Press and Red Dashboard has published *Words For the Deed*.

Dustin Pickering (Book Review: *My Glass of Wine, The Reverse Tree, and Healing Waters Floating Lamps*) has been published in *Seltzer, Writers on the Rio Grande*, the virgin Muse for Women anthology, *Vagabonds*, and *di-verse-city* 2013. He will be in *di-verse-city* this year as well. He was a Special Guest Poet at Austin International Poetry Festival, and a feature for Public Poetry in 2013. He owns Transcendent Zero Press with his partner Z. M. Wise. Together, they publish the print journal *Harbinger Asylum*.

Fred Pollack (Poetry: "Lethal Injection") is the author of two book-length narrative poems, *The Adventure* and *Happiness*, both published by Story Line Press. A collection of shorter poems, *A Poverty Of Words*, February 2015 from Prolific Press. His work has appeared in *Hudson Review, Salmagundi, Poetry Salzburg Review, Die Gazette* (Munich), *The Fish Anthology* (Ireland), *Representations, Magma* (UK), *Iota* (UK), *Bateau, Main Street Rag, Fulcrum,* etc. Online, poems have appeared in *Big Bridge, Hamilton Stone Review, Diagram, BlazeVox, The New Hampshire Review, Mudlark, Occupoetry, Faircloth Review, Triggerfish,* etc. He is adjunct professor of creative writing at George Washington University.

Larry Singer (Essay: *You Spin Me Right Round*) lives in sunny Orange County, CA. He has been a quadriplegic since 1988 and every day has a new story to add to the autobiography he is working on. His injury has never held him back, as he completed his doctorate in clinical psychology in 2002. His prior published works include "Wheel of Misfortune", an article about trying out for Wheel Of Fortune published in *New Mobility,* and "Psychological Aspects Of Acceptance to Spinal Cord Injury", his dissertation. He currently works as a tutor at the Santa Ana Public Library Teenspace. He hopes one day his story will inspire and motivate others to live life to the fullest.

C.W. Spooner (Short Story: *Moral Imperative*) has penned stories that appeared in *The Storyteller* and *Spitball -- The Literary Baseball Magazine.* He has published *'68 - A Novel,* and *Children of Vallejo,* a collection of short stories. His collection of essays, memoirs, poems, and reviews titled *Yeah, what else?* will be released in February, 2016. He is currently working on a second collection of short stories, tentatively titled *Tales from the O.C.* He lives and works in Aliso Viejo, CA.

Allen Frederick Stein (Poetry: "Emily's Eyes") teaches at North Carolina State University and has had two stories published in *SNReview* and one each in *Aethlon* and *The MacGuffin.* He's had poems published in *South Carolina Review, Southern Poetry Review, Aethlon, Modern Age, Roanoke Review, 5-2: The Crime Poetry Journal, Juked, Cape Rock,* and *Leviathan.* He has two poems forthcoming in *Modern Age,* and one each in *Juked* and *Aethlon.* His poem "Edna Pontellier Undrowned" has been nominated for the 2015 Pushcart Prize.

Anca Vlasopolos (Book Review: *Late in the Day*) has published over 200 poems, the poetry collections *Penguins in a Warming World* and *Walking Toward Solstice*, and the non-fiction novel *The New Bedford Samurai*. Most recently she published the poetry collection *Cartographies of Scale and Wing* (Avignon Press, 2015). She is Professor Emerita at Wayne State University, where she taught English and Comparative Literature for 39 years and now lives with her husband on Cape Cod.

Will Walton (Poetry: "One for Addie") lives in Georgia. He has a BA in Creative Writing/Poetry from Valdosta State University. His poetry has been published in *IthacaLit, The Oddville Press,* and *Odradek*

Barry Yeoman (Three Poems) was educated at Bowling Green State Univ., The Univ. of Cincinnati, and The McGregor School of Antioch Univ., in creative writing, world classics, and the humanities. He currently lives in London, Ohio. His work has appeared, or is forthcoming in *Red Booth Review, Futures Trading, Danse Macabre, Harbinger Asylum, Red Fez, Vine Leaves Literary Journal, Crack the Spine, Burningword Literary Journal, Two Hawks Quarterly, Broad River Review, Soundings Review* and *The Rusty Nail,* , among others. Recently, he was a finalist for the 2014 *Rash Award in Poetry* hosted by *Broad River Review*. You can read more of his published work at www.redfez.net/member/1168/bookshelf

Essay

Raymond Chandler
by Wayne Christeson

In 1948, in *Harper's Magazine*, the English poet and critic W.H. Auden wrote:

> [Raymond Chandler's works] are serious studies of
> a criminal milieu, the Great Wrong Place, and his
> powerful but extremely depressing books should be
> read and judged, not as escape literature, but as
> works of art.

Well, in all deference to Mr. Auden, there is nothing depressing about Raymond Chandler. And though received criticism pigeonholes him as a "hardboiled" writer, there is nothing hardboiled about him either: he is about as different from Dashiell Hammett, who truly is hardboiled, as a three minute egg is from a ten minute egg. Chandler's novels are far richer than mere detective stories, and when he is on his game, which unfortunately he sometimes isn't, he is as good as almost any other American writer.

In many respects Chandler is the equal of Hemingway, whom he often burlesques, or Thomas Wolfe, or other writers of his era. In subject matter and ease of style he may be closer to Scott Fitzgerald. The reason Chandler is not more highly regarded is that he didn't write symbolically or allegorically, or about serious subjects like war or politics—or bullfighting. And he didn't see himself as a "literary" figure.

What Chandler did was create a detective, Philip Marlowe, who is one of the strongest and most genuinely likeable figures in fiction. And he sustained a steady evenness of tone for Marlowe's character over a period of almost twenty years. That's not easy.

Marlowe is dismissed by critics as a simple cynic, but he is actually a wry and clear-eyed observer of full-bodied Americans who find themselves in desperate situations. His characters are substantive and human in the sense that they often do not fully recognize what they are doing and, in fact, that they are fooling themselves. They may respond to their plight with cowardice or mendacity or even brutality, but it is unusual for one of them to be purely evil, unleavened by complexity or humor. Chandler's characters have something about them which is genuinely sympathetic because he is able to juggle the ancient complements of tragedy and humor without becoming absurd or unrealistic. The power of his characters grows from the rich complexity of good and bad, dishonesty and stupidity, which afflicts them all.

Marlowe tries, sometimes at considerable cost, to maintain his moral integrity in a world of these people, and for the most part he succeeds. But his integrity is based on a code of honor and discretion which is peculiarly his. His integrity may require him, in the end, to look the other way, or to bury part of the truth in order to save someone's reputation or illusions about himself, which in Marlowe's eyes are often the same thing. In his own way, Marlowe is a realistically forgiving man: there is almost never a clear triumph of good over evil in his life, for he recognizes life for what it is. Marlowe's life is an exact and exacting application of American flexibility and pragmatism.

Chandler was classically educated at Dulwich College in England, but he spent his working life up until age fifty in the Southern California oil business. He lost jobs continually to a combination of heavy drinking and womanizing, and he lost his livelihood altogether when the oil boom petered out. When he had nowhere else to turn, he began writing pulp stories for detective magazines like *Black Mask* and gradually realized that he could write well. He did not publish his first novel until he was almost fifty, and that novel was one of his best, *The Big Sleep*.

The Big Sleep was so fresh and American that Hollywood decided to make a movie of it with Humphrey Bogart and Lauren Bacall. It's not a bad movie—with the voice-over at the end: "What did it matter where you lay once you were dead? In a dirty sump or in a marble tower on top of a high hill? You were dead, you were sleeping the big sleep ..."-- but the best film of a Chandler work may be the Robert Mitchum version of *Farewell, My Lovely*. It's not surprising that it's so difficult to catch the complexity of Marlowe on film, but it's odd considering how deeply the movie culture informs Chandler's work and how effortlessly cinematic his writing is.

Chandler was too drunk to write the screenplay for *The Big Sleep*, so the studio brought in some other screenwriters to try to salvage it—most notably William Faulkner, in his brief and misbegotten fling with Hollywood. There is a story, and a telling one, about how the screenwriters reached a point in the plot where they could not tell what happened. So they called Chandler and asked him. Chandler was on a bender at the time, and he said he would get back to them. When two weeks had passed and Chandler had still not called back, the studio called him again, and this time he admitted, "You know, I'm not really sure about that myself."

True or not, it is a telling story because it illustrates how little concern Chandler had for plot. Character and atmosphere were everything to him, and if the plot made sense, all the better. In typical Chandler fashion, he said once that his operating principle was, "If you reach a point where you don't know what to do next, have a man walk through the door with a gun." He didn't write like Dorothy Sayers.

The beauty of Chandler's writing—and its fun—comes from the combination of his graceful classical style and his foreigner's love for fresh, rough American language. Look, for example, at the beautiful, panned-in moment with Anne Riordan from *Farewell, My Lovely*:

> I put the light on her face and she blinked. It was
> a small neat vibrant face with large eyes. A face with
> bone under the skin, fine drawn like a Cremona violin.
> A very nice face.

"Blinked" is the critical word here, briefly freezing the scene like a snapshot. The Cremona violin is characteristic of Chandler's famous similes, but it isn't just facile wordplay. It emphasizes the taut strength of the curved bone finely drawn under Riordan's delicate face; it connotes airy, vibrant openness behind the face which resonates with the power of fine music, expressed through her widened eyes. "Drawn" extends the reach of the simile into the tight, astringent stroke of a bow across the violin's strings, or a knife across the throat. The scene momentarily stuns Marlowe, as surely as it does Riordan, and it seizes Marlowe's romantic perception of beauty. But then he steps back, and with purest irony he adds, after a cinematic caesura, "A very nice face."

3

Cynical? Hardboiled? No: there isn't any question about how Marlowe feels about what he sees.

Or look, in the same story, at the first scene between Marlowe and Lindsay Marriott. Marriott's fey, abstracted, not-to-be-bothered pose—"The effect was as phony as the pedigree of a used car"—betrays the fear and indecision of a soft gigolo who, as long as it is easy and relatively safe, works his weak but deferential charm on wealthy women. Chandler establishes Marriott's character in his uncertain movements, punctuated by his inconsequential, legato dialogue, while Marlowe remains for the most part imperturbable and still. Marlowe can sense that Marriott will end badly: Marriott braces his back against, of all things, the curve of his grand piano, like a parlor warbler. But Chandler never makes Marriott a figure of fun. Marriott is flawed, weak, sad, and at the end of his rope. After he dies, Mrs. Grayle says, "Poor Lin. He was rather a heel."

Marlowe's character is established in the same way, though more in his distanced internal perceptions than in what he says and does—which are often the ironic opposite of what he feels. It is clear from his professional but wryly disgusted attitude toward Marriott what kind of man Marlowe is. Yet from the quietly lyrical descriptions of the house above the sea, Marriott's flowers and the car he drives, Marlowe expresses his observer's distance, his dispassionate ability to penetrate the silly ostentation of Marriott's things and see their beauty—"The big foreign car drove itself, but I held the wheel for the sake of appearances". These are not cynical or sarcastic perceptions: they are clear-eyed and wry, regretful that beauty should have come to this. His thoughts are truly compassionate, for Marlowe carries compassion in his heart, no matter how cruel or fraudulent people may be. In his heart he is a romantic who seeks after redemptive qualities in the harshness of his world.

In a famous essay, "The Simple Art of Murder," Chandler concludes:

> In everything that can be called art there is a quality of redemption ... But down these mean streets a man must go who is not himself mean, who is neither tarnished nor afraid ... He must be, to use a rather weathered phrase, a man of honor, by instinct, by inevitability, without thought of it, and certainly

4

without saying it ... The story is his adventure in search of a hidden truth, and it would be no adventure if it did not happen to a man fit for adventure.

Chandler was for many years admired as a serious writer overseas. Marlowe's idiosyncratic code of honor made him a natural object of interest for existential analysts of "radical freedom" like Sartre and Camus, though Marlowe and Chandler would certainly have scoffed at that. But finally, as Chandler's legacy has matured, American critics have begun to recognize the beauty and importance of his writing. He has recently been chosen by the Library of America to be included in the pantheon of America's greatest writers and re-published for permanent preservation along with Hawthorne and Melville and Henry James, and all the rest.

Chandler would have been amazed, and Marlowe would probably have responded with his wry best to Auden's over-blown opinion—something like, "What the hell is a criminal milieu?" (though Marlowe would certainly know). Or, to steal a phrase from *Farewell, My Lovely*, "If there's A Great Wrong Place, Mr. Auden, that's me you hear ringing the doorbell."

Poetry

Three Poems by Barry Yeoman

End Of Summer

Holy hell knows we can't stop time
as wasted days propel dark clouds.
Families argue in their cars
while the dire ill are hooked to tubes.

Psychotic minds suffering paranoia
join petty squabbles at insane asylums.
Help us now as never before
these days unravel in empty rooms.

Birds array on an electric wire
to groom and think before feeding again.
Our stomachs growl with hunger too
as we fire up grills and flip our burgers.

Ignorant neighbors cuss and fight
over cellphone minutes and cigarettes.
How populations progress at all
is beyond the doubts of unwed mothers.

They hold babies and push the others
as streets grow crowded with obese
loners. We race against the power of
light, to get ours before things fall short.

Soon enough the weather turns nasty.
Flagpoles clang in the spitting snow.
Downs Syndrome kids soil their pants
as broken mothers cry in corners.

Parking Garages

I remember climbing
the open stairwell
of an old concrete parking garage.
Bottle caps and cigarette butts,
some fluttering candy wrappers
in corners. The echo
of car doors being shut,
sometimes the glimpse of a driver.

The squeal of tires,
squeaky frames
in need of lubrication.
Bouncing metal plates
that guarded deep potholes
as people left the crumbling structure.

Then, an eerie quiet.
A respite from the noisy streets.
These stark city spaces
matched my mood as a child.
Think of a concrete maze,
of jazz music, and Edward Hopper.

We walk like ghosts
through our reflections in glass.
Who's to say who we are?
Our lives are grim photographs.
In the checkout lines of stores
we avoid eye contact
with strangers.

The newspapers are almost obsolete.
A dead body removed

from an apartment complex,
where will it be reported?
What happened, who was it,
what does it matter?

Recently,
A hospital parking garage
in Denver,
the day before surgery.
Unusually warm for February.
70 degrees and sunny
on top of the six-story lot
where I climbed a stairwell
to get a better view
of the mountains.

Photo by cellphone
didn't do them any justice.
Same with catching a fine bass.
It never looks as big in the photograph.
It's all about the experience,
the presentation, the hit!
The fight to land the startled fish.

Then, released, and gone.
Like so many days
in parking garages
where the hollow ranges
of our quirky lives
are lost without climax.

Back home,
listening to jazz,
I hear distant applause
in a concert hall
on an old recording from Paris,
made long before I was born.

High keys of a piano
pound a menagerie into my earphones
on a sub-zero Ohio morning.

Hanging On

Winter hangs on
like an angry pit-bull,
entrenches the spindly trees
with snow.

Green tropical plants
are in my imaginary garden
next to a deep blue sea.

Battery mates
have already reported
to spring training.
The smell of grass and leather,
pop of the glove,
crack of the bat.

Memories for a moment
before the barren landscape
of the North
brings back
the raw reality.

Time hangs like icicles.
No movement
to the stingy season.

All attention turns

to internal things.
Maladies magnify themselves.
The body looms large
shacked up from the cold.

Steam escapes each breath
on rare outings.

Temperatures dive
to the negative digits
and we wait.

The kind of waiting
that turns the mind
into a black slick.

Thoughts won't stick,
jump from nonsense
to memory
and back again.

Just hanging on
is an empty proposition
when time stands still.

The sky is a pale window
in life's solid block.

Poetry

Two Poems by Cristine A. Gruber

Clock

The clock in the kitchen
was always five minutes fast,
an imagined buffer to fool us into
believing we were ahead of schedule.

But we weren't ahead, not really,
for the moment we looked up
and said those inevitable words,
"we have five more minutes,"
we invariably set ourselves up
to be late for whatever event
lurked just around the corner.

I thought it was normal to live this way,
until I spent the weekend at a friend's home,
and the family was preparing to watch
their favorite evening program.

I instinctively looked up
at the kitchen clock ticking away
like a ceramic time bomb,
and reflexively said, *"five more minutes."*

My friend just stared, and continued
to wonder why I was always late.

To the Manner Born
For Marina

At the age of three she preferred grapes to candy,
apple slices to chocolate chip cookies. By the age
of seven, she was appalled to learn that chicken
McNuggets were made from actual chickens. At
ten, the pork chop was passed over for the pasta.
And at the age of twelve, the sight of blood on the
Saturday evening steak turned her stomach to stone.

I suppose I should have picked up on these and
other clues, though the word, vegetarian, was never
used until she left home for college. Settling in, she
ate the sugars and the starches and gained the typical
Freshman fifteen. But she continued to turn away from
the presence of meat, happy at last to have full control.

Born a herbivore, but forced to be untrue for the sake
of the misguided, insisting they knew best in how to
provide a balanced diet. But there's nothing balanced
about hormone-packed meat and puss-filled dairy. Of
her own volition, she intuitively knew how to feed her
body right. Plant-based at birth. To the manner born.
Her right to health achieved once she finally left home.

Book Review

The Translator by Dah
Transcendent Zero Press (2015)
Reviewed by Michael Minassian

Dah shows his skill and a careful craftsmanship in his latest collection of poetry, the aptly named *The Translator*. This collection is a rich journey into the mind and words of the poet. From the moment I stepped into Dah's poems, I felt I was entering a place of magic, memory, and sight. Questioning his place in the universe, and sometimes answering, the poet seems to be seeking a moral compass to navigate through the world. In the title poem, "The Translator" the speaker hints that the poet and poetry can help us find our way:

> in between there is a message
> that we can neither locate nor decipher
> and we can only hope that it surfaces on time
> with a proper translator

The "You" voice, the sensuous feminine voice that speaks in the poems, suggests answers, some of them uncomfortable truths, about life and death and the mutability of existence. From the excellent poem, "The Moon's Deep Wounds":

> You said: 'Maybe life is an invalid
> or a guide gone astray and inside each
> circle of breath there is a path of light'

The speaker doesn't linger in the grip of melancholy and the reader is able to see the "path of light" as images of hope appear near the end of the poem:

> We hear voices coming from along the river,
> children's delicate voices, gentle laughter
> happiness the color of autumn

Yet the reality of existence is its non-permanence, and the speaker's lingering fears and doubts creep into the last stanza:

> and the wind shifted to a steady chilled motion
> You shuddered in silence.
> Overhead, the noisy geese made their escape
> and every leaf was shaking.

Throughout the book, the poet seems to be asking the question: How do you translate the natural and sensory world so that it has meaning. In many of the poems, the reader gets a sense of place and the contemplation of what is seen and heard. And the poet's other self, the constant "You" of the poems provides a touchstone through this journey:

> Your face, your open eyes
> thrive in memory, mythology.

In one of my favorite poems in the collection, "Harbor Scene" the poet uses fresh images and metaphors to paint the landscape and give the reader a window to the natural world. In the penultimate stanza, the young couple is briefly introduced and painted in bold strokes, anchoring the poem in the physical world:

> a young couple presses into each other's warmth
> the way noon shadows press into hot adobe walls
> as the imposing air from autumn's icy saturation delivers
> a tight aching emptiness seldom known by lovers

My only complaint about the collection is that a few of the poems are printed double-spaced, rather than single-spaced as the majority of the poems. I'm not sure if that was the poet's intent or a decision by the publisher, but I found it distracting and felt it didn't add to any of the poems in question.

Throughout the collection, Dah's poems explore the natural world around him: the earth, sea, sun, and wind and the creatures, large and small that populate it. Through his poems, he explores his inter-relationship to the natural world and probes it for meaning. Sometimes this leads the speaker in the poem to recognize the negative side of human behavior. But there seems to be a hope to tame the negative impulses with kindness and compassion. He does this through graceful poetic metaphor such as in the poem "We Are Only Sleeping":

> We must hold tight to the harmony/that is left...
> words of love in the cockpits of our mouths,
> dive bombing, softly dive bombing

Often, I was startled and moved by an image such as the opening lines of the poem "Dust"

> What we think about
> is our motion
> almost never our stillness

What Dah has created in these poems is a space for us to think about our own stillness and in that stillness to drink in his poems and savor what is contained.

Poetry

Side Door Blessing by Mike James

Side Door Blessing
    for Jesse Breite

find a rock big enough
to fill the biggest hole

then find the biggest hole
and fill it

wait for a shower of dirt
to cover that rock

plant some weeds
in the fresh dirt

bring along water
for a mud pie

gather other,
smaller rocks

build a house to guard
against the *big bad wolf*

spend nights making candles
of various colors and scents

befriend the town's witch
even if it takes a full winter

let her recite fairy tales
beside your hearth

if she makes you the hero of any story
know she is the one

Book Review

Late in the Day by Ursula K. LeGuin
PM Press, 2015
Reviewed by Anca Vlasopolos

Late in the Day, the title of Ursula Le Guin's most recent poetry collection, sounds a valedictory note that is borne out only by a few poems in this astute, incisive, wide-ranging book that is beautifully designed and fits nicely in the hand. I expected no less than to have my breath taken away by a writer whose works I've admired, learned from, and taught for several decades. This book did not disappoint.

I will not discuss the masterly prosody of these poems since Ms. Le Guin herself does so in her *Afterword*, where she even lists the poems in the book by form, for the convenience of readers unfamiliar with quatrains and sonnets, free verse, etc. Her exacting method—"By free form I mean a discernible pattern"—if followed by people professing to write free verse would elevate the genre above the abuses into which it so often falls.

The erudition and passion that underlie these poems make them a discovery and joy to read. Each thematically selected or prosodic section becomes a journey into complexity. Both *"Relations"* and *"Four Lines"* are reminiscent of Neruda's *Odas Elementales*, poems that zero in with minute attention on the seemingly ordinary, the every day, the object of use: "a tool" that by sonnet's end becomes "this weight that wants to fall and, falling, sing." "The Salt" is an equally stunning four-line poem that sums up earth and its beings. The last section, "The Old Music," takes us to the beginnings of poetry—folk songs, ballads, hymns—yet with this poet's inimitable imprimatur: an "unblessèd" America where no "god or priest" rules; a medieval Sir Thomas whose pursuit of the "gleeful Happy Beast" ends in defeat.

Brought up with Greek mythology as my nightly going-to-sleep tales, I was surprised and moved by Le Guin's version of the Eurydice-Orpheus myth, in "Hermes Betrayed." The poem begins with a stanza quietly announcing a supposed fact: "When a god grieves/ the deep

stones/ at the four corners/ of the world tremble." That Le Guin
celebrates Hermes/Mercury, "airy, jaunty," should not come as a
surprise to those of us steeped in her writings: she's always seen the
trickster, the go-between worlds, the bi-being as attractive since that
foot in both worlds allows such a being a more rounded, more
encompassing vision; Coyote and the protagonist of *Always Coming
Home*, to name but two, attest to this authorial affection. Yet in this
poem, even Hermes of the "cool aplomb" is betrayed, as is his charge,
Eurydice, for, as "The burden of his deathlessness/ weighed ever less/
at every step of that/ brightening way with her," it's the poet who
"turns" and breaks the god's only chance of learning mortality. And
though Hermes, given his nature, "would not grieve," "the deep stones
shook."

There are devastating statements on the lateness of the day:
one such is "Disremembering," where the specter of a body that goes
on without its mind is as chilling as it gets: "the soul plods onward to
no end." Yet this is a book that celebrates life, its last word a
benediction upon our much-benighted earth: "dancing." If there is a
cluster of images that dominates this collection, it's stones—their
stillness and silence, which the poet prizes. In *Late in the Day* Le Guin
herself to some extent embodies her own character, Stone Telling,
showing us through this great variety of utterly mastered poetic forms
the way home.

Poetry

Three Poems by Rodney Nelson

Declaratory

dig into the black prairie and
find yellow clay or ride to the
uncommon sand pit
        another
ingredient from its sea time
and admit that what swam up here
lived for something and for nothing
    what buzzed
in a much-later June
        what snorted
and bred or ran to
the hunt
   what jumped off an oxcart
to till and hay and milk
      that all
lived for something and for nothing
   did it only
to go around
with a go-around that happens
to be Earth now
      that none of them
was an interloper on it

Prime Acres

I looked at a field and it looked back
in one of my beginning days which
might have gone on to another and
another in a gradient run
of morning after morning in June
up to where I am waiting now but
I am only a part of the man
the field foresaw
      the string got broken
and walking in the sight of many
an outland has made me remoter
yet that part is still on the edge of
the first field in bindweed and the scents
of hay and morning go to my quick

Accompanied

it would not have a face or a name
      or a nature
so I do not look
but can sense it in the grayed painting
on the wall of the tavern and at
the room's dark end where it may have moved
      be waiting now

      I should not go out
to watch them smoke and talk
      or at all
but it wanted me to even though
it could have sent me to any park
or to my chair because it is here
within me and will move when it moves

Short Story

A Matter of Honor
by Joe Giordano

I'm Dimitri, and I trade under the radar throughout the Mediterranean. When I arrived at Jayden Zammit's complex in Valetta, a uniformed guard stationed inside a black gate checked my Greek passport, and I was admitted. I hadn't met Zammit, yet he responded to my fax inquiry with a dinner invitation.

Zammit stood at the entrance of an oak door. He wore a designer suit, was tall, in his sixties, with black eyebrows and gray hair over his ears. Although it was a cool night, sweat glistened on his forehead.

"Thanks for the invitation."

He gave me a wry smile and escorted me into his dining room. A Murano chandelier hung over a table for twenty. Silverware and china inscribed in gold, "The Consulate of Iceland," glittered in the light. It took me a moment to realize that there was a swarthy man sitting at the opposite head. He had a black mustache, was in his mid-thirties, and wore a jacket with an open collared shirt. He leaned his cheek on his hand and evaluated me with dead eyes. Zammit made no sign to introduce us so I sat.

"You have a magnificent home."

"Thanks, but it's too big for me. My wife is deceased, and my children live in the city. Do you have family?"

"Only me."

Zammit glanced at the dark man.

I picked up a plate. "What's the meaning of the engraving?"

Zammit snapped open his folded napkin. "I'm the Consulate General of Iceland in Malta. I posted a substantial bond, and they appointed me." He placed the linen on his lap.

"The prestige must be helpful in business."

"Normally yes."

"And the gentleman at the other end of the table is your personal security?"

"Not quite."

A balding servant in a black outfit served us three bowls of *stratiatelli* soup.

The man said, "*Buon appetito.*"

Zammit looked up. "Ah, Signor Lucchese has entered the conversation." Zammit leaned back. "As you know, Sicily is near enough to piss on. Signor Lucchese was *persona non grata* in Palermo. He smuggled himself into Malta and took sanctuary with me."

"He's a friend?"

"A business acquaintance."

My eyebrows rose.

Zammit put down his spoon. "Signor Lucchese convinced me to give him residence in my home. He emphasized the good health of my children."

I stiffened. "He's the reason I was invited to dinner?"

Zammit spread his hands. "Malta is too close to Signor Lucchese's enemies. He wants to settle in Greece and take up his sundry business activities."

Lucchese interrupted. "*Una faccia, una razza*, one face, one race. Greeks and Italians are simpatico, yes?"

"And how am I supposed to get him into Greece?"

"I own a sailing yacht. Two men are needed to handle the craft. Signor Lucchese is an accomplished sailor. I assume a Greek can handle himself at sea. You can make Piraeus within a week."

I folded my arms.

Zammit's eyes widened. "I understand what I'm asking is extraordinary. As a down payment on our future relationship I will sign ownership of the boat to you. A diplomat is a good friend to have."

I pushed away the soup. "Get somebody else to ferry this *mafioso.*"

Lucchese pulled out a black revolver and clunked it onto the table.

I rose. My chair fell backward and smacked the floor. I clenched my fists. Lucchese eyed me. My mind calculated how fast I could close with him and the utility of a butter knife against a pistol.

Zammit was stern. "Put that damn thing away. We're negotiating."

23

Lucchese flashed me a grin of crooked teeth. He shrugged and shoved the revolver back into his shoulder holster.

Zammit tugged at my sleeve. "This house is Icelandic territory. Police will not enter the gate. Please, let's not have trouble."

I felt a pounding in my chest. A trickle of sweat rolled down my back. I took a long breath, picked up the chair, and sat.

"Let's not argue. The boat and fifty thousand euro wired to your bank in Greece."

The alarm bells in my head could've woken the dead. "The answer is still no."

Zammit slumped in his chair.

There were footsteps, and a woman in her early twenties entered the room. She had brown doe eyes, long black hair, and wore a short sleeveless blue dress.

I swallowed.

Lucchese frowned. He raised his hands in the air. "You said I'd handle this." He smacked his palms on the chair arms. "Signore, this is my sister, Azzura"

I stood and smiled. "I'm Dimitri Andreas, *piacere.*"

Azzura revealed pure white teeth. "Piacere." She sat across from me. "My brother is too full of pride. He prefers threats to honesty." She shot a glance at Lucchese. He looked down. She transfixed me with eyes that glistened with moisture. "Signore, my brother and I are in peril. We need your help. Would you reconsider and take us to Greece? *Per favore?*"

Had I ever seen a woman as beautiful? Okay, I thought, her brother's a *scifoso*, but Azzura has been caught up in some affair not of her making. Lucchese needs me to get them into Greece, so I'm safe for now. I'll find some way to get the revolver away from him. I took a deep breath and turned to Zammit. "How do they get past the border police?"

"They have been issued Icelandic documents."

I nodded. "You will wire the money before we leave?"

Zammit's face brightened like a sunrise. "Most certainly." He called out to his servant. "Bring Miss Lucchese some soup."

The sound of a sailboat cutting through the open sea is silence.
Lucchese was at the helm. "Ready about."

24

Azzura ducked under the boom like a barefoot cat. Her bronze legs were muscled like a dancer's.

"Helm's alee."

She released the working sheet. The boom slipped to starboard, and I winched trim the lazy sheet until the telltales were straight out.

Azzura's hair rippled in the breeze under a white cap. She wore her orange life vest over a cobalt blue two-piece.

Lucchese wore the same tattered tee shirt with an Italian flag on the front since we started. He had the pistol in his shorts belt. I hadn't packed for sailing. I made do with jeans rolled up to my knees.

I looked at Azzura and sighed. Lately my life was tread worn women, casual sex, and waking headaches. Azzura was young and beautiful, but she was also loyal. Family was important to her like it was to me in the Eden of my youth, unsullied, real. I wanted to talk to her, but what wouldn't sound contrived? I anguished over how to begin, and after a few clumsy attempts I settled for small smiles when I caught her eye. I worried that she thought me an adolescent-minded flirt. Why the hell was I kidding myself anyway? I was too old for her.

Lucchese and I took turns at the helm sleeping in four-hour intervals. Azzura stayed awake while he slept, so there was no chance to grab the revolver. We were making great time and were about twenty-four hours from our destination.

As the day cooled toward evening, I saw towering clouds roll toward us with a sneer. My gut soured. I pointed. The muscles in Lucchese's jaw bulged. Azzura's eyes widened. We attached jack lines to our waists. I helped Lucchese furl the sails. He sidled toward the helm and started the engine. I crouched below the wheel. Azzura hugged the base. Her scent was chocolate and blood orange. The wind rose and rattled the metal boom. My mind refocused on the oncoming storm. Flags and rope riggings snapped like whips. The green white-foamed sea levitated the bow skyward then plunged us down, and the horizon disappeared. Rain pelted us in horizontal sheets. I tried to shield Azzura with my body. She pressed her face to me. She was warm. The clouds blotted out daylight. Lightning flashed and illuminated Lucchese in a bright frozen image like a match strike. Thunder exploded overhead. His hand lifted from the wheel to shield his eyes. The boat lurched, and he lost balance. He tottered backwards and tumbled over the transom into the sea. Instantly his jack line snapped off the deck and stretched like a rubber band. I jumped up and took hold of the wheel.

Azzura's hands went to her head. "Oh my God, Salvatore." She pulled my arm. "Help him."

In the strobe of lightning flashes I saw Lucchese floundering in the heavy seas. We rolled, and I slipped to my knees.

Azzura tugged on Lucchese's jack line in vain. She shouted over the storm, "Save him." Her top was soaked and revealed the outline of her breasts.

"Take the wheel," I said.

She struggled on the slippery deck, got to the helm, and hugged the wheel. I took hold of Lucchese's jack line, pressed my feet against the transom for leverage and pulled. The boat dove into a trough and a huge wave washed onboard and hit me in the back like a rabbit punch. My head hit the stern. Azzura was washed into the wheel-well and came up sputtering. I tasted blood. My hands had loosened, and the gain I'd made on Lucchese's rope paid out. I took hold and restarted the tug of war against the sea. My back strained. I pushed with my legs and stretched to make headway. The line cut my fingers and palms, and I cursed the lack of gloves. Hand-over-hand I reeled him in. My biceps and thighs burned with exhaustion. I saw Lucchese's hand clutch the transom. I tied off his jack line on a cleat, reached over the stern, and grabbed his belt with both hands. I hauled him onto the boat and tumbled backwards. He retched and vomited seawater. I crawled to take the helm from Azzura. She said, *"Grazie,"* in my ear, and her lips brushed my cheek. She went to her brother on all fours and cradled him. I kept the throttle at slow power. It seemed an eternity before the storm passed and was a growl in the distance. My fingertips touched the echo of Azzura's lips on my face.

***

Sunrise and a cloudless sky that blended into a blue Mediterranean opened my eyes. Lucchese's head lolled, his back against the port side. He was unarmed, and I expected the revolver was lost at sea.

He lifted his hand to me. "Grazie." He sounded like his throat was filled with ground glass.

I nodded and swallowed. My mouth was cactus. I got us both some water. Azzura was below deck.

"Why did you save me?"

I shrugged. "I didn't want you in my nightmares."

Lucchese chuckled.

"Can you get up?"

He nodded.

"Let's get underway."

Lucchese struggled to his feet. We got the sails up, and I cut the engine. I was at the helm, and Lucchese plopped down next to me.

"The Italian police are after you?"

Lucchese waved as if shooing a fly.

"What did you do?"

He gave me a sidelong glance. "It was a matter of honor."

My eyebrows rose.

Lucchese puffed out a breath. "Nunzio Puglisi took an improper interest in Azzura. He was shot in front of the *teatro* in Palermo's Piazza Politeama. The police were not the problem. The Puglisi clan marked me for death, and there are more of them than grapes on a vine. One day while I walked in the fields or on the street or sitting on my mother's porch, a Puglisi would take his revenge on me. Then one of my family would need to respond."

"Vendetta."

"*Si.* A friend smuggled us into Malta."

"But you threatened Zammit's family?"

"Zammit is no innocent. You approached him for smuggling, yes? But he's no Sicilian. I pressured him, and he folded like a deck chair."

"Why did you drag Azzura into this?"

He gave me the crooked tooth smile. "We need to tack." He rose to his feet.

Lucchese was at the helm when I sighted Kithira. I sang out, "Land ho."

Azzura came on deck and shaded her eyes from the sun. She turned toward her brother and nodded.

Lucchese's face clouded. He held up his hand to her. "Dimitri, you won't turn us in to the Greek police, will you?"

27

"Why would I?"

Lucchese looked at Azzura. "I told you."

She lifted Lucchese's revolver and pointed it at me. "We can't take the chance."

I took a step backward and raised my hands. I glanced at Lucchese and then back at her. The barrel drew my eyes like a magnet. It looked like the mouth of a giant cave. I considered trying to wrestle the pistol away, but she'd shoot before I got to her.

I said, "You don't need to do this."

Azzura cocked the revolver. Her eyes were like a cobra's before the strike.

I heard gulls overhead, the creak of the boat, and the sound of my short breaths.

Lucchese stepped forward. "He saved my life."

"He saved you because of me. There's a longing in his eyes when he looks at me."

"That's love, Azzura."

"They all want love. Papa wanted love."

"I fought Papa and took beatings for it, didn't I?"

"That's when I couldn't take care of myself. Now I can."

"Azzura, I took the blame after you shot Puglisi."

"That was honor."

"There's another way."

"Is there?" She leaned against the boat. Two hands held the weapon.

"Let him swim for shore. Maybe he makes it, maybe not. But we have time to sail into port, and he's no danger to us."

Azzura didn't move. "He'll talk to the police when he gets ashore."

"And tell them what? We'll have Greek identities very soon. Azzura, I owe Dimitri a blood debt. Per favore. Don't dishonor me."

Azzura's eyes flickered. She sighed. Her gaze softened, and she uncocked the revolver. "Okay Dimitri, go for a swim. Maybe the Nereids will save you." She gestured with the pistol. "Go ahead. Jump. Now, or I'll forget the debt my brother owes you."

***

You'd think an eight-kilometer swim would cool me off, but when I think of Azzura, a tingle runs up my back. If she was damaged in her youth maybe love is the cure. I sound like a ridiculous romantic, I know. But there was something in her eyes when she let me go. It wasn't only her brother's honor. Anyway I need to be sure. I've inquired about them in Athens. Maybe they're in Thessaloniki? Men who've seen Azzura won't forget her. It's just a matter of time before I find her.

Poetry

Three Poems by Darren Demaree

Nude Male With Echo #256

Incurious about the string
that offers almost freedom
to my physical world

I jumped off the roof
of my house to prove a point
to my wife; I can be broken

& live long after that
breaking. Our tether
is as thick as our gravitas.

Nude Male With Echo #257

It doesn't matter
that the edges are sharp.
You are cut on entry.
You are cut in transition.
You are cut into pieces
when you exit.
One dove bleeds on our faces
& that doesn't matter
either. We are born
with adrenaline
& that means we will
be allowed to play God
in a few scenes. So,

30

all of the roles are ours.
The landscape chooses
a costume for us
before each day opens
& that is the best
I can explain waking.

Nude Male With Echo #258

The light escapes,
does whatever it wants
& that is why it's warm.

To be ecstatic
& cold would break
every law of physics.

Essay

You Spin Me Right Round
by Larry Singer

The big event of the day began innocently enough, but that's how they always start, don't they? The words that started everything were "Stat Counter", but they could have been any of the other 1,025,109.8 words in the English language that provided the opening salvo to today's adventure. I was trying to tell Billie how she could get good stats for her blog. We were at the Writer's Roundtable but the only round table was the one I was sitting alone at, moved to be within earshot of everyone else at their square table. It's not that I didn't want to sit with everyone else. It's that it is not as convenient for me as a circular table. My big power wheelchair doesn't fit that easily due to the joystick, arm rest, and casters. Whereas most of the time, I'm just "Larry", at least to myself, it's times like that, where I have to sit at the "kids table" that the reality of my disability, a quadriplegic, floats to the surface, and I am "the disabled guy". Mind you, that was a minor reminder, compared with everything else that happened that day. As a matter of fact, it was so minor, I didn't think of it til just now when I began writing about the rest of the day's events, all of which served to remind me thatI'm disabled.

Upon reflection, Alexander had just one horrible, no good, rotten, lousy day to contend with, and Lemony Snicket's series of unfortunate events were child's play. No...when life has its way with me, the struggles are of Jobian proportions.

So, "Stat Counter"... Billie and I were trading notes on our blogs, mine a rare music blog and hers a collection of letters from Vietnam. I was attempting to give her tips on driving up traffic to her blog by way of linking with other blogs found in Stat Counter stats. I turned on my chair as I had done countless times already that day, without incident, and rolled to her to show her something on my iPad. When I got close, it happened. At first it seemed like nothing. Oh, I rolled over something, or I'm caught on this chair leg, or anything else other than "my wheelchair is frozen and will not move". But that's what it was. My chair was frozen on the left side, so it made my chair

32

continually veer to the left in a spinning movement. It was as if Billie was Magneto and when I got closer, she disabled my chair's motor. And of course, when it first happened all my twisted mind went to was a vision of androgynous lead singer Pete Burns of 80's one hit wonder band Dead or Alive singing their one hit "You spin me right round baby right round..."

I had no time for that, as I had more important things to think about....like Stat Counter. And as my mind is apt to do when crap happens, I start counting the stats of all the unfortunate circumstances that have happened to me, and do a compare and contrast to see which was the most unfortunate. Was it the time the power steering hose blew in my van on Walnut St. at 11 pm? The tow truck driver, avoiding all contact with me wanted to know if "he could get in the cab". After informing him I was fully capable of speaking for myself, I also let him know that I am permanently stuck in the chair. Flexing his mental muscle, he asked if "he can get on the floor". After informing him again that I am capable of speaking for myself, then I informed him of the even higher unlikelihood of me getting on the floor. So then, this Einstein said that since it is illegal for me to ride on the back, if I see a cop on the freeway, "just duck". Even though, according to MapQuest, we were 36 miles away, when we arrived at home at 2 AM he demanded $129 because the 48 miles he calculated were 8 miles over my allotted 40. It was too late to argue with this extortionist, but when I contacted Dodge Roadside Assistance the next day, the MENSA member of a customer service representative's explanation for the discrepancy was because the tow truck had "bigger tires".

The executive lunch crowd started getting bigger at Panera. People were passing by wondering why this wheelchair person was sitting alone in the middle of the restaurant with no tables around him. A couple of people sitting nearby kept looking up and staring, holding themselves back from moving to help. And then my mind wandered to Aldrich Park at UC Irvine, where I was zipping through the park to class and my caster came flying off after hitting it with the cement cracks created by an uprooted tree. And after sitting with my head between my knees for about 5 minutes the sweet young petite girl who was studying in the park finally realized I wasn't doing a down dog and asked in her soft voice "ummmm...do you need help?" Unless she was a collegiate Wonder Woman, it was going to take some brawn, which came in the form of the three burly football players walking through the park. They righted my upper torso and lifted the chair and put the caster back in its socket, but the rest of my day consisted of rolling the wheelchair equivalent of tiptoes, hoping the caster did not slip out of the now insecure socket.

Above the din of the yuppie crowd was Panera's piped in Muzak...a mix of non-threatening, soulless, generic "quiet storm" music programmed to appeal to the widest audience. And there it was...Michael Jackson arguing with Paul McCartney about whose girl it was. This meisterwerk in banal, insipid pop pablum, which fit in perfectly with Panera's intent of having aural innocuity was all my mind needed to get the neurons firing along the synapses in my brain. When this started, my mind started clicking through the Viewmaster of "Larry Singer's series of unfortunate circumstances" and settled on a single frame...a snapshot of Michael Jackson spinning while grabbing his crotch. What does Michael Jackson have to do with my story? The last time a side of my wheelchair froze was the day Michael Jackson died. This was my "where were you the day JFK was shot?" moment...the day Michael Jackson died. And that day I was spinning circles in the living room of my house. I couldn't even make it out the door to catch the bus, so we had to rent a van. When we got to the shop, the technician informed us I needed a new motor, which would take 7 to 10 business days to arrive from Ohio, but this was a long holiday weekend so add 2 days to that. The next stop was another shop to get a rental for the downtime, but this was a longshot since they were a scooter shop. They did have a chair, though it looked like it was last used to transport the infirm around Bedrock Memorial Hospital. Because life can never give me my fill of misfortune, I definitely left my mark on the shop while during the transfer the clamp on my urinary drainage bag flipped open and the contents emptied on the floor.

Michael Jackson beat it out of my thoughts when I remembered I had more important matters to tend to. That memory did remind me of a cold hard fact...repairs like this won't be done in hours or days. It may take weeks or months. I focused on what I had to do for the next few weeks, and seeing how ferociously active I am, it was a lot.

So there I was, at Panera, with three relative strangers who were there to talk about writing, not do makeshift wheelchair repairs.

One of the "strangers" happened to be one of my doctoral instructors when I was in graduate school but, dammit Jim, he's a doctor, not a mechanic. I generally tend to be an extremely optimistic and "silver lining" thinker, but my score on the LOT-R (an optimism/pessimism measure) was skewing to the "P" side. My mind emptied, all I could see was the worn carpet in front of me and the front door, 50 feet away (a far distance to travel in a 500 pound chair that doesn't move), which would lead to the two tiered ramp, leading to the parking lot, ultimately leading to my van. Oh, and damn, there's that entitled idiot who parked his handicapped placard equipped SUV over the crosshatch making the turning radius in to my van more tight. But why was I bothering with these pie in the sky thoughts? Getting INTO my van wasn't possible until I was OUT of Panera. My mind should probably tend to more immediate concerns, like should I have a freshly baked croissant or a blueberry muffin when the morning crew comes in and wakes me up?

So the group came over because, bless their hearts, they thought they could do SOMETHING for me. My 26 years of experience informed me there's nothing that could be done. I know that they are all very competent writers, but writing me a new ending wouldn't be in the cards. An act of God would help, maybe. I did give them the benefit of the doubt that maybe there was SOMETHING that could be done, and had them check the clutches, which are easily accessible. Nope...all in order. Then they started firing suggestions about maybe pushing my chair or putting me in one of Panera's chairs...but that aforementioned 26 years experience....it knows all too well about the viability of any of that happening. No, my ONLY chance, and a snowball's one at that, was finding a wheelchair repair shop in Orange County, and one that could handle electric wheelchairs, and one that was available RIGHT NOW, and one that could come and do a repair in the field, and one that would be able to do said repair with me in the chair. To take total poetic license and mix metaphors, my chances now were finding a needle in a snowstack in hell.

I hit the phone and called the closest shop I knew (coincidentally about a mile and a half away off the freeway). I explained my dilemma and wasn't expecting a miracle, and the receptionist said she would see if she could reroute someone. I spent the next five minutes on pins and needles anticipation, and when she came back on the line, the lift in her voice encouraged me. She was able to reroute the tech. He would be there in 20 minutes. Thoughts of warm morning baked goods dissipated in my head as I had a small glimmer of hope. I then realized the reality of the situation...sure I had a tech coming, but if he didn't bring a magic wand, or a crane, there wasn't a lot he could do. At the very least, someone would be there that spoke "wheelchair".

After we hung up, my phone rang with a number I didn't recognize. I answered thinking it was the tech. It wasn't. It was Brinks home security calling to let me know the glass break sensor has discharged...in my house.... 10 miles away. With me stuck in the middle of Panera. I called my wife and explained my dilemma and had her go home to survey the situation.

After sitting motionless for 30 minutes, suddenly the door opened and I was momentarily blinded by a flash of light coming from above. When the rods and cones in my eyes settled, I saw him.... my savior, a guy in grungy jeans and a white tee holding a toolkit and searching around the dining area. I called him over, and he got right to work. He assessed right away, the left drive wheel was stuck. He searched deeper and found the cause of this inactivity was the control module in the motor. He knew he had a spare motor back at the shop, if it was the correct one was a different story. Plus, the most important element, I couldn't be in the chair. Many people who are similarly injured have a helper with them at all times for such situations. The price of independence for me is that I have no such thing. I put out APBs to my caregivers to get some on-call assistance.

Assistance, of course, would only be needed if I made it home. There was still the matter of getting to the door, down the ramp, across the parking lot, to my van, up the ramp (still with the tight corner, thanks Mr./Mrs. Entitled), and then being turned with a tighter corner and pushed in to my driver's space, ensuring lockdown in the wheelchair lock below me. My savior started to push, but he may as well have tried pushing a tank. A couple onlookers who had seen the events taking place and sensed that something was awry offered their services. My chances now improved exponentially. One of them got the idea to put something under the paralyzed wheel to allow it to skid. They got a plate and put it under. Doing a sign of the cross at this point would have been warranted, but, being Jewish, I opted for a Star of David. On the count of three I moved more in the next 20 seconds than I had the entire previous 45 minutes. The plate, made of plastic, was designed for light salads, not 500 pounds. 15 feet and the first one broke. They went and got a second while the lunch rush of 25 onlookers stared in astonishment at what they were observing, wondering how they were going to tell this story so their coworkers would believe them.

Four broken plates later, my Samaritans somehow managed to get me from my stagnant position in Panera and in to the drivers space of my vehicle locked in place. I said my thanks and they wished me well, and I closed my van door. The battery died in the chazaride, so I needed a jump. Then my mind wandered to...my bladder? Yes, I just remembered one thing I should have done BEFORE becoming permanently stuck in the driver shaft of my van...empty my urinary drainage bag. The little child inside me embarking on a cross country road raised his hand and said "I gotta go!" I figure if I could potentially get stuck in the van, I had to make room in the bag. Luckily my sister lived close by and luckily she was available. I made the trek to her place and 20 cc's at a time with a torn Styrofoam cup, she emptied it for me. Then, my stomach told me that the muffin I had at Panera was not sufficient to sustain me. My sister brought me an assortment of snacks that you stock when you have growing boys and let me have some.

In the interim, one of my caregivers, Mady, returned my text and said she could help. Her office was literally right across the street from the shop. I thanked my sister and was on my way. I scooped up Mady and we went across the street. We got to the wheelchair repair shop and I had her go in to get someone. The repair guy came out and informed me that they couldn't do anything with me in the chair. He told us to go get some "furniture movers" from 99 Cent Store and he would show her, my 110 pound caregiver, how she could move me. Given the ordeal three strong men had in getting me in to the van...it wasn't happening. I contacted the Irvine fire department, and they said that they could totally help me, so we headed home. They arrived five minutes after we did. The jaws of life were not necessary, but they came up with a plan to pull me out of my van and place me in my spare chair. Luckily I had a spare in the garage, though its battery hadn't been charged in a while. It had just enough juice to get up my ramp and get into the driver slot to take Mady back to her office and my chair to the shop. I made it there minutes before closing, and I waved the chair goodbye as I watched them push it in to the shop. It is industry-standard to never make promises other than "We'll call you when it's done", so I left with ambiguous feelings of hope.

Luckily, I now had wheels to get me from point A to point B, granted, the battery indicator showed that I had the petrol fuel tank equivalent of about 1/8 of a tank left in the current charge cycle. I thought about tomorrow, whatever point b's I had to go to since I "might" get a call letting me know that my chair will be ready. I thought about the act of God, albeit less extensive than today's, that would need to occur to pick up my chair, take it home, and get me in to it. So I checked my calendar and realized the greatest irony of all...I had an all day workshop scheduled on *Teaching Resiliency to Children*. Add another stat to the counter.

My first point B this day was to stop at the market to pick up milk. After visiting the dairy case, I confidently rolled towards the register and realized just how clear my head was not being plagued with thoughts about being stuck and sleeping in my van. The barrenness of my mind allowed other thoughts, like catching the glimpse in the corner of my eye of the big orange machine I just passed by. Then I saw, of all people, Clint Eastwood. There he was, Dirty Harry himself, saying to me "you've got to ask yourself one question: 'Do I feel lucky?' Well, do ya, punk?" Well, Clint, as a matter of fact, if I told you about my day, even you would say I was lucky. What more could go wrong? I turned toward the orange lottery machine and had a clerk insert my $20 bill. Scratching the tickets off later fit in perfectly with today's theme of some luck colored by a lot of misfortune...I "won" $4. What luck.

Book Review

My Glass of Wine, The Reverse Tree, and *Healing Waters Floating Lamps* by Kiriti Sengupta
Hawakaal Press, Moments Publication
Reviewed by Dustin Pickering

Waiting in the Garden of Eden

I read Kiriti Sengupta's three collections *My Glass of Wine, The Reverse Tree,* and *Healing Waters Floating Lamps.*

My Glass of Wine advocates a return to religious principles and compassion. The author truly believes the world left sane compassion and sweetness when it began to deny the truths of religion. Sengupta discusses everything from namesake to the Bhagavad Gita in this prose and poetry collection. Lately I have noticed a new form of literature being written by Indian writers. A combination of prose and poetry that mutually complement one another is emerging from this sacred land where literature is honored and adored. *My Glass of Wine* fits this category and is a national bestseller. We are first introduced to Sengupta's key concepts in this small volume.

His work reads like an exploration of life—seen from the Yogi's angle—and an acceptance of its universality and uniqueness. We are taught that Yogis meditate to bring the Mother to the Father, a metaphorical journey that describes the climb of energy up the spine in meditation. Much of Sengupta's imagery stems from this symbolic process.

There is one odd poem in *Healing Waters Floating Lamps* called "Fish-Lip" that seems to have caught the Foreword writer's attention as well. It turns from the imaginative and accessible to the strange and uniquely personal symbolism presented by the author. In this poem, I am reminded to review the opening thoughts of the book:

"On the ascending shoots
Your fear matures
A few apprehensions as well
Your roots hold it tighter

39

Desperately deeper

And much deeper rests your God"

This reminds me of the poetry of *The Reverse Tree*. I am also brought to the Biblical proverb, "The fear of the Lord is the beginning of wisdom." Wisdom is distinctly universal and perennial in its goodness. Much life is lived before it presents itself and is brought to the light. Fear is what brings us closer to our deepest values; we feel the world tugging at our Selfhood, wanting to avenge its confusion; and, we cling tighter to our sense of Self as our roots are exposed upward. *The Reverse Tree* is an extended metaphor for human nature, a life of service, and just how strong we, as people, must become to expose our graces toward others. "With service evolves dependence, and honestly, it is the ladies who turn out to provide better shade than the men," Sengupta opens in the first chapter. Why then is the tree commonly conformed to men? Being flows through all things like water and wisdom is the greatest joy. Sengupta quotes the Bengali of Tagore, "I envisioned the external through the light of my eyes." The Soul is God Himself, so the light of the eyes is the revelation we experience as we live. The Soul is Master, Commander, and the lens through which we perceive our golden glories.

I think a bit on the Garden of Eden and the allegory it presents in light of this book. Much of the myth's imagery can be reconciled with the Guru's meditation metaphors. Adam and Eve as Father and Mother, but the Mother turns away instead of rising up toward the Father. She is "tempted", perhaps distracted, by a wise and clever serpent. This serpent is assumed to be the Devil in traditional interpretations. Perhaps the snake is rather a symbol of the spine, and this allegory reflects the very same wisdom as holy India's religion! The Mother turns directly to the spine, and takes its advice to eat the fruit (the core of the head where the Father and Mother meet), and the result is the expulsion of the couple—yet they are expelled as one, in unity. The snake is forced to consume dust—recall the dust that accumulates on our self-image. Adam and Eve have already attained wisdom but are now guarded from picking the fruit of the Tree of Life. This Tree is protected by a young angel with a flaming sword. This is symbolic of the process mentioned in *The Reverse Tree*: "Removing agony from life is not an easy task unless we recognize the source. This is all about the worldly attachments that we grow knowingly or unknowingly…" Even the great Sufi poet Rumi explores the tarnishing of Self by worldly attachment. Our humanness is distinct in worldly attachments. They are why we live.

Why does Eve turn from Adam after all? In Genesis 2:7, there is a pun on the Hebrew "Adam" and "adama"—adama means "ground." It is woman, Eve, a reflection of Man, who turns him from the Garden and worldly pursuits to knowledge of good and bad. Adam is a reflection of God in his dominion over the fertile plain, yet he is evicted from his paradise and punished with death. To know good and evil is a death itself, the "sickness unto death", the separation of Self and Other, and the hesitation we experience in our apprehensions. God, wise and primal, tricked the original couple by putting the pieces in place—expecting them to learn the powerful lesson they would only understand from experience. A very similar expulsion and detachment occurs during Adam's sleep when Eve is brought from his rib. We are taunted with reminders of our origins we cannot understand. Things aren't ideal for this very reason. We learn distinctions. We learn judgment, the very vice the Savior advised us to harness. The cherubim and its revolving sword of flame, mentioned in Genesis 3:24, are acknowledgements for the insatiable quest of humankind to find permanence and its ultimate truth of origins.

Sengupta, page 36 of *The Reverse Tree*:

> *"and the wounds surface again*
> *in all directions…*
> *sporting the guise of youth…"*

Is he not reflecting the same paradox?

Eve, mother of all living, is cause of our mysterious life and our long thirst for paradise. She was the first to survey the land and truly seek dominion in ways her husband could not imagine. She implores him to remember her birth so he can find himself. *She* was the one in true service to the betterment of humankind by fulfilling human destiny, and leaving a legacy of wonders.

Poetry

Lethal Injection by Fred Pollack

Lethal Injection

The needle missed Diaz' vein. +24
minutes, still moving; licked
his lips, "blew." "Grimaced."
At an unspecified time, they found
the vein, injected
more "cocktail." Death
at 34 minutes plus change.

Conservative blogs joke:
"Go for an hour." Quote
a fictional guard: "It's gotten
harder since the ACLU
insisted that we can't perform
CPR. We used to push them
right to the limit, then bring them back.
It brought such joy to the families
of their victims."
More thoughtfully: "Screw the people
whining about the 34
minutes. Why aren't they pissed that it took
27 years for this murderous scumbag
to die? He took up
27 years of the people's money ..."
"Maybe if Joseph Nagy
had been properly armed and trained, Diaz
would have been killed in the robbery."

You have to admire the on-demand
hate. Liberals
don't hate effectively, we

despise – the equivalent
of eros, love of an inferior;
hatred parallels
agape, the love of what's above.
Otherwise, it occurs to me
I began writing –
arcane, meditative stuff – the same year
Diaz visited that topless bar.

Cartoons by Allen Forrest

Artist's Statement

Painting is a cross between a crap shoot, finding your way out of the woods, and performing a magic act. Each time I begin to paint I feel like I am walking a tightrope—sometimes scary, sometimes exciting, sometimes very quiet, and always, always surprising; leading me where I never expected to go. Doing art makes me lose all sense of time and place and go inside one long moment of creating. Whenever I feel a painting in my gut, I know this is why I paint. The colors are the message, I feel them before my mind has a chance to get involved. Color is the most agile and dynamic medium to create joy. And if you can find joy in your art, then you've found something worth holding on to.

Allen Forrest
Artist/Cartoonist

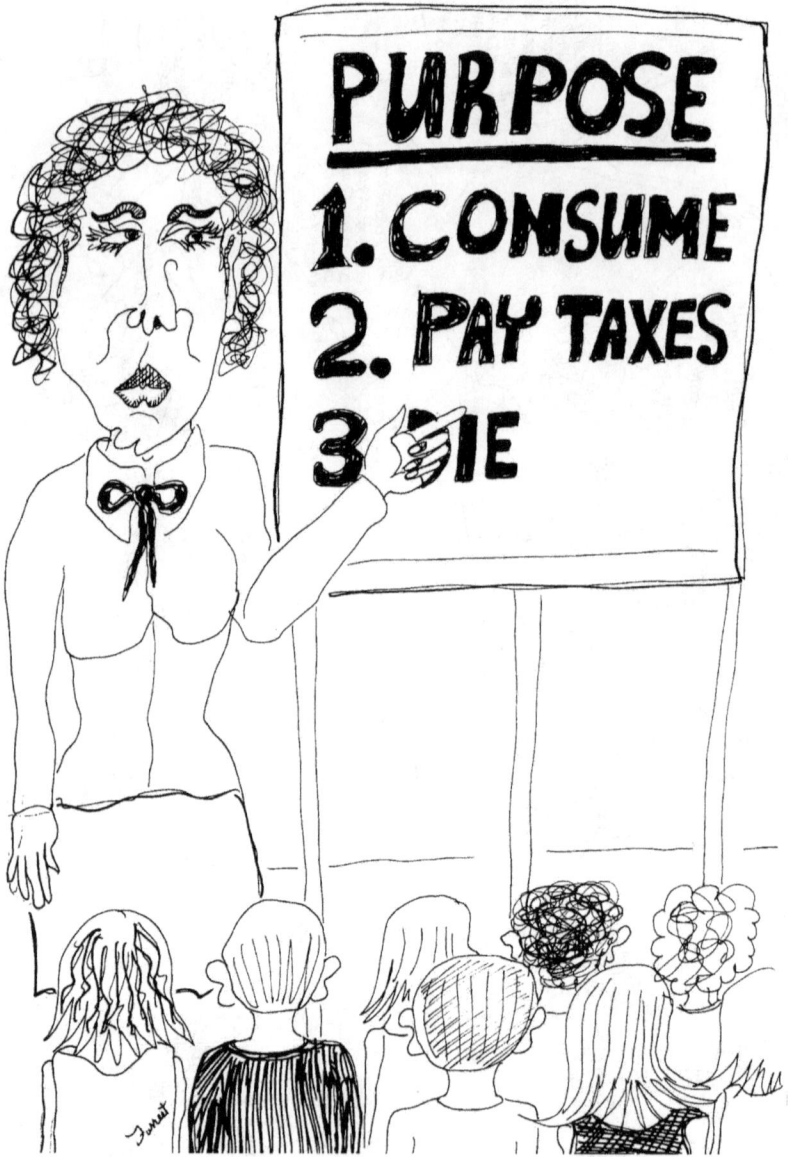

Essay/Prose Poem

Orange County Seafood
by Charlie Keys Bohem

Have you ever eaten Orange County Seafood? You start with bread and butter. Sometimes it's rye, sometimes white, sometimes a baguette you have to rip apart with your teeth like a Geek at a chicken. There are wines. There are a lot of wines because people come to restaurants like these with the idea of spending a lot of money. There are also some beers, always summer beers and usually Blue Moon, and some cocktails. Then there's the menu, which is a list of stock items - a house salad made of crunchy, tasteless iceberg lettuce with the option of several salad dressings including but not limited to: a ranch that tastes mostly like sour cream, and an Italian with an unsettlingly sexual consistency - unrealistic and more in the vein of "impossible amount of bodily fluid" hentai. Oil and vinegar is your best bet. There are steamed clams in salt water with a buttery oilslick on top, crab and shrimp cocktails, crab cakes, and a lot of different fish that have all been filleted and cooked down into generic white food matter. The fish come with sides like steamed greens, which sometimes try to choke you and stick in your teeth, which isn't good if you're on a date. Also steamed vegetables, and mashed potatoes. Your date will probably order the vegetables and the greens and you'll feel guilty eating the potatoes. The fish ascend in feudal tiers from very cheap dab to unlisted market prices you don't find out until you get the check. Lobster and tuna are the king and queen of the seafood section. The check is usually a fantastic sum when you compare it to the size of the dabs, or the tuna brick. This is especially true after desert, which is chocolate cake with a scoop of ice cream. You pay the check and then you go home, and find out maybe that you got scombroid poisoning from tuna that sat out too long and accumulated histamines shit out by a bacterium that thrives in heat. When they cooked the tuna, all of the bacteria died, but the histamines remained in tact, and the posthumous spite of a hundred thousand dead microbes gives you a synthetic allergy attack for a couple hours until you fall asleep. Otherwise, if you don't get scombroid, you feel fine, you feel full, and you go home, maybe with your date. It wasn't disappointing. Anywhere else you could have eaten is fifty miles away, too, because the county is like a little butter spread over a million square miles of bread—bread you have to tear apart with your teeth, like a geek.

Poetry

Three Poems by Nels Hanson

Sure Thing

I was trained on the northern bank
of the fast Kings River near Laton

all one Central Valley warm spring.
Thoroughbred, I raced as three year

old, county and state fairs, Fresno,
Sacramento, before Bay Meadows

and Tanforan by cold Pacific. Then
south to Hollywood Park, Del Mar,

Santa Anita on to Mexico's Agua
Caliente, way eastward to Florida,

Hialeah in silver air-cooled trailer,
New York State's rainy Saratoga.

Derby at emerald Churchill Downs,
Preakness at Pimlico, the Belmont

Stakes, last meet for Triple Crown.
I didn't run first any race of three,

second, third, second, photo finish,
before I was put out to sweet grass

and seed. With one hundred dams I
never saw I sired one hundred foals

49

I never knew. I haven't raced, worn
bridle, head stocking, saddle, borne

any rider in years. In standing sleep
I don't replay loving cup, horseshoe

of red roses at my neck in winner's
circle, bolt at open gate, bell trilling

electric from battery, blink at flying
turf, smart whip, silken flashing arm,

take sugar cube from happy jockey.
Blue-black ponies dash homestretch

head-to-head, my colts, fillies, rider-
less. All take the lead, overturn rails

and beat far odds to escape forever,
or nose to tail in unbroken ellipse fill

oval wire to post. No track MC calls
Big Race, bookies their morning line—

Players pick trifecta, bet no Place or
Show but always each horse to Win.

Walking Home

Sometimes the boy of 12 trailed
his laughing friends, isolate, raw
with unshared hurt, school-day

sting, hidden shame. Talk grew
faint, cruel and far as air around
his head turned black with dots,

swarm of wingless faceless flies,
trees strange now, hanging leaves
knives and his shoes dim useless

things on a littered street. Despair
opened its trapdoor, endlessly he
was falling, feet-first down a well,

the secret part in him folding on
itself, eyes waking everywhere.
Melancholy, golden sunset's last

green whisper, said goodbye and
night's gigantic face approached,
broken piece inside him breaking

last time, softly. He tasted poison
tears, hope forgot, all that might
have been, then giving in to death

grave's sadness lifted. A different
light appeared, cobalt sky pressed
close. Ash trees caught fire, puzzle

bark stood clear. Glass trapped in
asphalt flashed, lit up, trumpets
calling. Breathing rescued air he

recognized his place and hurried,
picked wrappers from pavement,
crushed cans soiling holy ground,

raced ecstatic cleaning resplendent
avenue he ran alone, only one who
realized they walked again in Eden.

Back From the Castle

In arduous dream becoming nightmare
a towering staircase of spiraled stone
with no warning shifted, turned upside

down and I descended, pushed hard by
furious wind, nearly falling headlong
miles into Earth, over treeless wastes

to deserted city. Center stood a castle
howling with rabid wolves. Hundred
desolate halls I traced the roar against

my will, led to an innermost chamber,
final, circular, where mad-eyed tyrants
of History flailed screaming, shackled

by long chains to stanchions anchored
in one round wall. Each murderer just
out of reach of all the rest still fought

to grasp, strangle his vicious brothers,
him, now him, then another in a ring
and reaching none. Faces bulging hate

ten thousand years appeared identical.

Twin shards of a single looking glass,
every profile mirrored the other's fury

there wasn't slack to kill, forged iron
links reining tight last instant to annul
attempted suicide. When millions die

slayers always count one body missing,
disappeared, guilty cause escaping his
death, ruining all until the end of time.

Poetry

Two Poems by Carolyn Gregory

Body Awe

Opening like a book,
ribs fly buttresses unzipped to lungs,
stomach and heart,
vivid with capillaries,
a new form of art
where plastics and design merge.

A skeleton lassos rope,
the head shown with three faces,
an eyeball prominent
above well-formed teeth.

Two acrobats are locked like lovers,
gluteus and calf opened
as if for barbecue,
the male's feet splayed like a reptile,
his shoulder raised to hoist the woman
curved like a dolphin without flesh.

Whatever faint flush fed us
on a hot, sticky day,
not fanned well in dark inner space,
sweating turns to awe
at the coordination
of organ, skeleton and skin

shining with millennia of evolution,
ready to step out of these glass boxes
and fly!

Old Masks

"I have already lost touch with a couple of people
I used to be." —Joan Didion

Like the girl with hair hanging,
a long throw of blonde
thrown down her back
who slept with local rock stars
unsure of what to do
with all that inner motion,
she is back there in Boogieland,
listening to Joe Cocker wailing

and that other woman
married with all her bottles
hidden in a half open closet
dreaming of a Sorrento
music box from an old trip,
the one night stand in Venice.

Old masks must be scrubbed
with strong powder. each pulled off
like a dead bandage
that no longer fits.

Poetry

Owled by Craig Evenson

Owled

Clean dishes and bedding
for what

I've hidden

where I find myself,
a cat in a woodpile,

there the handhold required
        your one tearless eye
to claim victory

in the absence of a stream
to bear away the drainage

Numbly humming
Nina Simone

the sun

the woolen drawl
from something
you've long
been tempted
to cross the center line
into

                you can't see the stars anymore
                not even here
                you should write a poem about that

Short Story

Sylvia
by Billie Kelpin

I never saw her smile—not once—not in all the months I would come to know her. Her eyes held something. I didn't know what. It wasn't vacancy. It wasn't sadness. Maybe it was rage—maybe hidden, seething rage. Maybe that's too strong. She was the most homeless-looking adult student who had ever walked into my classroom. The jacket she wore the first night had the unmistakable look and smell of Goodwill. Her slacks were dark plaid and polyester and the navy blue of them seemed to seep up into a haze that enveloped her, extending outward into an almost visible aura around her edges. Her hair was dark, her eyes were dark, and as she stood in the doorway she seemed dark...and lost. She had the look of a child who had just awakened upside down in an overwhelming large bed. She was wearing neither hat nor gloves that night, but she wasn't shivering. And silent. She was definitely silent. Not the silence of the other deaf students in my class. Not the silence that is willingly broken to make hearing people understand. This silence was different. It seemed purposeful like the closed mouth silence of a person holding something like liver that was too disgusting to swallow and too large to spit out.

She arrived late that first evening, and I could feel myself trying to be gracious for what I knew would now be, at the very least, a ten-minute disruption. It wasn't anyone's fault. It was a deaf culture thing—a social phenomenon that swoops in like a wild fire in a forest parched by the need to be understood. Most of the students in my class had at one time attended the Wisconsin State Residential School for the Deaf in the 60s. Seeing an old classmate now, some 30 years later, would start a blur of concepts that would flash laser-like across the room on visual strings that begged to continue in vibration. And in the blur, all news would be told ...*Remember JK, senior year?... new job...g-r-a-p-h-i-c-d-e-s-i-g-n... Really? ... You?...twins?...cool!* (the latter signed like deaf kids in the 60's used to sign *neat*).

57

I didn't mind the anticipated interruption. I wasn't any longer the young "hearie" teacher who would catch but a few signs here and there, missing the subtleties like a tourist in a foreign land. I was into the field long enough to feel one with this culture, like the American Jesuit in Guatemala giving his homily in Spanish or the British importer in Beijing ordering lunch in fluent Mandarin. I had even dreamt one night in only signs.

But there was no interruption this night. No flashing lasers across the room...only sign-less stares at the reticent navy blue figure who still stood in the doorway.

"Welcome," I signed, "Come in." I hoped I was smiling as I gestured to a vacant chair.

"Your name?" I signed as she sat.

Only three finger-spelled letters later—"S"... stop... "y" stop..."l"—and I knew, and my class knew, that our group dynamic was about to change. There was none of the deaf style fluidity of fingers that makes unspoken words become calligraphy in space and time. Some thirty-five years old and she was clearly new to signing. *Perhaps she had been late deafened? Could be hard of hearing? Raised orally without signs?*

'S-y-l' continued, struggling for the next letters like a child at the piano looking for the keys. In the slow-motion of the waiting, my mind started playing with the possibilities...*Sylvester?* I laughed to myself. *Sylvania....yeah, like the light bulb!*... No, obviously it must be Sylvia...*Come on, Sylvia, paleease get it out.* She continued: "v-i-a".

"Nice to meet you, Sylvia. Do you have a name sign?"

Sylvania's eyebrows knit as she just sat and looked at me.

Name sign! I thought. *Damn, she doesn't even know what a* name sign *is.* I turned to the class hoping for help. One by one my students spontaneously illustrated the concept of their own name signs; Sylvia barely blinked in response to their efforts. Finally, we agreed that Sylvia would now be an "s" at the temple, and I hoped she caught on. Class that night felt long. Sylvia's lack of understanding was forcing me to switch back and forth from an ASL deaf-preferred signing structure to a more hearing mode of voiced Signed English in the hope that she might understand.

And I resented it. For the last two weeks, the profound deafness of this particular group of adults had propelled me to a peak

58

experience. We were signing adult to adult, not teacher to child. And I was "in the zone," my skills being challenged to their capacity... two finger-spelled letters here, and I would know the word... a flicker of movement there, and I could understand who did what to whom and why. Three hours of "saying" without speaking...three hours of connecting and feeling useful. I was the privileged hearing person let into a secret world, and now it had to change because Sylvia couldn't understand!

I was thankful toward the end of the evening that Joyce, the director of the *Deaf Bridge* stopped by to see how the students were doing. I could finally sit down and let her take over. Joyce stayed to talk after I dismissed the class.

"I see Sylvia showed up," she started. "She appeared at my office to register this afternoon."

(*Appeared!* It echoed in my mind. What an accurate word for how she had entered my class.)

"I haven't seen her other sessions," I replied. "She doesn't seem to understand much... or even lip-read for that matter. Just recently became deaf, I take it."

"No...uh, no. It's not an age or progressive thing. She's been profoundly deaf from birth. Her sister told me."

"What!? For God sake, Joyce, she doesn't sign or even lip-read. Where's she been all her life...in a cave? It's the '90s, Joyce, not the 1800's! She's well past thirty. Not *one* deaf student in the class seems to know her. Don't you think that's just a *little* odd?"

As I looked up, Joyce continued explaining that Sylvia's sister was the one who had found the Bridge. "She can never help Sylvia register because she plays cello or violin for some philharmonic orchestra."

"How ironic is *that?*" I interjected.

"The sister only flies in and out of town every so often, so she pre-registers Sylvia by phone. I've never actually seen her."

As we walked out into the Milwaukee chill, Joyce explained that Sylvia was raised down south somewhere...

"Arkansas? Tennessee?"

She didn't know. "Shows up for class every other year or so. Great writing skills, though."

"That's what I mean, Joyce. I had her write a few sentences. "No dropped -*ed* or -*ing* endings…Perfect subject-verb agreement. It's like she grew up hearing."

"Talk to her sister. Trust me, you'll have the chance. She's called Sylvia's teachers in the past. I'll give her your number, if that's ok."

I thought phone calls in the evening from concerned parents were over when I stopped teaching little ones, but now there'd be a concerned *sister* calling! Nevertheless, I replied, "Sure." The mystery of Sylvia was too intriguing to say no.

The next week, the wind off Lake Michigan howled only to the hearing, but chilled everyone indiscriminately. Still, there was full attendance at the Bridge. Even Sylvia showed up—again no hat, no gloves, no shivering. Again, she simply appeared almost ghostlike, as if up from the floorboards or down from the ceiling. Again, she frowned through the first hour and a half of idioms and verb tenses. At break time, the other students filed past her, fingers chattering. Sylvia stayed seated at the end of the pressed-board tables, alone. "Break time," I mouthed to her, larger than I wanted.

In slow, straight "hearing" English Sylvia signed, "I-am-fine."

It felt unnerving to scurry about finding transparencies for the overhead projector and checking papers with one silent, staring student left in the room. I forced the feeling of discomfort somewhere outside of my body and pushed the guilt for not engaging with her down to some place I knew I'd be visiting later.

When I arrived home after class late that night, the phone was ringing. I answered with my coat still on.

"I'm Sylvia's sister. Joyce gave me your number. I'm Diana." Her voice had the throaty-ness of sophistication and I could visualize her playing a violin in an elegant long-sleeved black crepe.

I tried to not sound tired.

"Ah…yes. So happy you called," and I jumped right in with, "I've been wondering about Sylvia."

There was something cold and direct in her "W*hy?*"

"I mean her educational background. She doesn't seem to understand when I sign."

"She hasn't had much…" and there was that kind of silence that the controlling leave open for those not brave enough to leave it alone.

"Much?… schooling?"

"No, not much schooling. We're from Arkansas." She continued with lengthened vowels that would seem to confirm that fact. "I wasn't around much while Sylvia was growing up, so I don't exactly know. I think she started school and then stopped."

"Oh, I see." But I didn't. *Not around much?* But I was too tired to go there. *New subject.* "I don't exactly know our goals yet."

"She wants to learn more signs," Diana offered.

"Yes, I see. But…I'm wondering if a class in *basic* sign language to begin with might be a better match for Sylvia right now. Our class focuses on the refinement of English writing skills and discussions of socially relevant topics." I felt a twinge of guilt for wanting my "deaf only" class back to myself.

"No," she answered simply. Her voice was firm and seemed to echo in a room that sounded hollow to me, perhaps a sparsely furnished apartment that she rented when in town, I surmised. Again there was the silence that seemed to force my response.

"Well, she doesn't seem willing to mix with the other deaf students. She sits alone at break and doesn't go out to the hall to try to mingle or get a soda or anything."

I thought I had misheard the sister's next response.

"She doesn't know how to use the Coke machine."

"Uhhh…" I was scrambling for meaning…"Excuse me."

"She can't count money. She doesn't know *how* to use the pop machine. I want her to learn that."

I was dumbfounded at the concept. It was obvious that despite her homeless look and novice signing, Sylvia was in no way lacking in mental capability; her written responses to my writing assignment clearly indicated that. *How does one get to be some 35 years old and not know how to use a Coke machine?* The other students in my class might have been deaf, but they were *only* deaf. Bob was taking night classes because he had an appetite for politics and wanted to discuss articles in *Newsweek* and *Time*. Bonnie was the mother of hearing twins. Her toddlers could sign and speak and wore Nike tennies and little jeans from the GAP. She wanted to learn to sign the nursery rhymes she had never heard as a child. Rich, the graphic designer, studied at the prestigious National Institute for the Deaf in Rochester, New York. His new role as President of the Milwaukee Deaf Club would require an understanding of Robert's Rules of order.

I tried to explain the writing and vocabulary goals I had for this class, but Diana was insistent.

"Sylvia *needs* to learn things. Surely you could find some time…"

Of course, I could. What could be so hard in teaching someone to get soda from a Coke machine—someone who didn't understand a single word I signed or said or mouthed or mimed—during the one break I had all evening!"

Instead, I answered, "I'll give it a try."

"Next week?"

God, this woman! "Yes, next week."

I started next Monday's class with a discussion on writing autobiographies. It would keep the group working while I pulled each person out to work on individual goals. I saved calling Sylvia to my desk until close to break time.

"Sylvia, your sister called me. She said you'd like to learn to use the Coke machine."

"What?"

I wrote what I had just said in her notebook.

Sylvia reached for my pen. Under my sentence she wrote, "My sister called you? What did she want?"

"Yes." And I pointed to the sentence above once again.

Sylvia nodded like an obedient child.

During break, Sylvia and I walked to the vending machine area. I took some quarters out of my pocket. "Twenty-five," I signed "fifty, seventy-five." There was the familiar look of Sylvia-confusion, but I proceeded. I pointed to the slot and motioned her to put the coins in. She wouldn't take them from my opened hand. *Oh Lord* ….

"Ok, Sylvia, I'll go first." I placed the coins in the slot. I heard the soda drop below. Sylvia still stared at the coin slot. I pointed down to the tray, grabbed the can, and put it on the floor so I could continue signing. I took out three more quarters and handed them to Sylvia. Again, she wouldn't take them.

Ok…start her off…damn… this is taking so long.

62

I motioned for Sylvia to press "Push Here," but hadn't expected her reaction. There was fear in her eyes and she backed away from the machine as if it would harm her. "It's ok, Sylvia." After looking into her eyes, the task seemed to take on more seriousness, and compassion overtook my impatience.

I pointed again and mimed the action of pressing.

I was hoping I didn't look like some missionary in Africa in the 20's delighted with myself for exposing this soul to civilization, but I might have had that look. Sylvia simply looked confused, but she came closer.

"It's ok, Sylvia. Press"

The Miracle Worker had first hit the cinema long after I had declared deaf education as my major and I never went into the field to be Anne Sullivan. That night, however, as Sylvia pressed the button and I pointed to the slot to where she hadn't heard the soda come out, I felt as if I was at the water pump spelling out w-a-t-e-r. It was a fleeting feeling because I was the only one sharing in the triumph. Sylvia never reacted, never smiled. Her frown lines only shortened a bit as she walked robot-like with her soda back to the room.

I was hoping Diana would be out of town playing her fiddle or whatever in some city far away because I was too exhausted to rehash the evening. But no, again, the phone was ringing as I walked in the door.

I was actually excited to relay tonight's victory. "Diana, yes. So glad you called. Sylvia learned to use the soda machine tonight!"

I suppose I expected back a "Great," "Fantastic," "Thank you, Ellen, so nice of you to take the time."

Instead, Diana, simply responded, "Good," and not taking a breath added, "She needs to learn how to ride the bus."

"Oh brother! Will this woman never relent?" I could hear a Dr. McCoy voice echo in my head, *"For God sakes Diana, I'm a teacher of the deaf, not a social worker!"* And the concept of *social worker* became the new rope I reached for.

"You know, Diana, I would be more than happy to set up a meeting with you and Sylvia and a social worker."

But Diana couldn't meet us at class, she said… her "schedule and all… not possible."

I suggested Mondays since she seemed to be able to *call* on Mondays!

Diana then raced her response along some convoluted trail of logic paths that circled back and around and lost me somewhere in the middle. I abandoned the social worker idea and ended up capitulating once again to Diana's plan. I would try to unravel the Metro bus schedule myself, I promised, and later would help Sylvia to read it. (I would have preferred teaching gerunds and participles.)

Sylvia missed class the next week and I was glad. As I mimed turning an invisible lock near my larynx, the sign for *not talking*, a collective dropping of student shoulders seemed to take place simultaneously. Like a secret member to a special club, I could now sign silently, fluently, to my deaf-only students. Everything flowed that evening and I felt released and connected, the way lovers do when it's good.

The next week I signed, "Welcome back," as Sylvia slipped in after class had begun. Students were finishing their autobiographies and I was introducing "Little Bunny Foo Foo" to Bonnie for her twins. Sylvia read her assignment and got busy writing her autobiography.

Just before break, I walked over to her desk and signed, "Finished?"

Still stoic, Sylvia nodded her head and motioned down to her paper. I pulled up one of the folding chairs and started reading. Her written English was simple, but mostly "straight" (as teachers of the deaf like to say) and would need little correction. I could tell that from the first two sentences. I'd read for content I decided. It was a decision I wouldn't have had to make for the content was such that I had never read in fifteen years of teaching.

I was born in Arkansas. My mother died when I was six. I think in a fire. I had two brothers. My first brother drowned in a lake. My father was yelling at him. I was in the boat. He fell in. John drowned.

I was aware of my head moving back and forth to retrace the page as if reading the sentences again would change their meaning. Sylvia lowered her head to look into my eyes as you'd look under a

64

shelf to see why it was not seated properly. She knew the sign most hearing people use for "what" and signed it under my face three times as if I had found some spelling error that she was sure she hadn't made.

Not looking up, I wiggled my fingers to sign "wait, wait" with only one hand and read on.

My second brother died from being shot in the head. There was a lot of blood. I saw pieces on the floor. I saw it. I think that was his brain. I want to learn sign language.

Is this possible? I looked at Sylvia. Her face was impassive, stoic, resigned; and in that incongruity there was congruity, and I had to assume the sentences were true. I could feel my chest release the breath I had been holding. I told the other students to go on break, and I sat down and looked directly in Sylvia's eyes.

"What?" she signed again, "What?" more insolently now like a teenager asking, "What did I do this time to get me in trouble?"

I looked in the pools of black-blue tar looking into mine.

"Sylvia, I'm so, so sorry." The "s" of *sorry* pressed the center of my chest as it circled slowly over and over.

Sylvia's eyes became more opaque, and her frown furrowed deeper in apparent confusion.

"Why? Why are you sorry?" She signed every word.

Perhaps "sorry" didn't make sense to her in this context, I reasoned, and I tried to explain.

"I mean, Sylvia…I'm sad," and I mimed pulling down an invisible mask of my face. "I'm sad this—this all— happened to you."

Again she signed, "Why?" as if she was becoming irritated, and for some reason, I could imagine her voice. It would be a low, raspy voice, I thought, with a sarcastic edge of inflection.

"This, Sylvia." I pointed to the paper. "This! Death." I signed it again. "Death…your mother….fire" And again…"Death…your brother…drowned," and again "death, your brother shot. I'm sad all this death, death, death happened in your life."

Sylvia's frown lessened, she moved back to the support of her metal chair as if relieved that was all.

"Why are you sad? Don't be sad," she signed laboriously. She shrugged again as if the story were about an insignificant sliver she had just described. She shrugged once more and finger-spelled "s-o". She continued signing words she knew, slowly and deliberately. "So? So what? So nothing. That's life." Don't look at it and it will go away."

The words she signed felt ice-cube cold with rigid straight corners—words, I thought, practiced over and over again, to cool hot grief. And the words in sign slapped me in the face and chilled my blood, and froze the moment in my mind.

I needed to explain what was most likely evident in my face.

"Sylvia, do you know that most people don't have this... this death... *all* this death... in their lives... Some death yes, but like this? No."

For the first time, Sylvia looked scared and I stopped. Somehow I felt like I was tugging on something fragile. *And who are we to be so careless as to break the silken thread that holds someone together?*

Coming home from class that Monday evening, I was spent. I went to the frig for the Chardonnay without even taking off my coat. As I reached for the glass, the phone rang. Diana barely waited for my "hello" before saying, "Sylvia needs to understand the bus schedule."

"We've gone over that schedule several times, Diana. It's just not meaningful to her. "

"She *needs* to get to her new psychiatrist on 55th Street."

"I see. Yes. Well..." That topic was over for me and I shifted the conversation, "Diana, Sylvia wrote an autobiography. I wanted to discuss that with you."

"What did she write?" Diana seemed concerned.

I hadn't had time to put my briefcase away and I quickly found Sylvia's paper and read it to her sister.

At the end, Diana simply replied, "It's true. That's all true. But that's only the half of it," and she began a story that seemed to belong in a movie no director would be daring enough to put on the screen.

"My father abused Sylvia from the time after my mother's death all through high school. It was August when we moved to Little Rock. He'd bought a small farm and kept her at home. He never registered her for school."

"Then she never went to school?" I asked.

"I can't remember. I think she did, some days, I think. I don't know. I wasn't there."

Wasn't there again. There was silence as my mind scrambled to fit those pieces together. It was Diana who filled the space before the solution came.

"He'd have sex with her in her bed and then go out to the fields. I think she was seven. He'd lock her in the closet so she wouldn't run away. There were wires on the doorknob. Electric wires."

I was getting sick to my stomach as the possibility of causation came to my mind. I could make no sound to even acknowledge I was hearing this story. Diana continued.

"He rigged it up so that if she tried to open the door, she'd get a shock. He left a light on, though. Thank God, he left the light on. There were books my mother had. There was a card with finger spelling that someone gave me at the State Fair one year. She would lie on the pile of shoes and dirty clothes and look up at the light bulb and onto her card. "S-y-l-," she'd practice. "

"You mean, the name on the light bulb?"

"Yes."

My stomach felt like it was at the top of a roller coaster that was ready to fall. I was surprised at my fear.

"He raped her... all through grade school....he raped her...different ways. He made her do things. He told her she had to be silent." Diana stopped and waited.

I couldn't speak.

"What?" Diana asked. It was a familiar *what* and gave me the feeling that she was lowering her head to look into my eyes.

"What?" she asked. "What's wrong??"

"Diana, it's just so...so...horrific. I'm shocked. I'm sad."

On the other end, I could hear a sigh, not of resignation, not of shared sorrow, but of relief. I could imagine her slinking back onto a metal chair relieved that that was all. I could almost see the shrug of her shoulders as I heard the words from a voice that *was* raspy and low with a sarcastic edge of inflection.

"Why are you sad? Don't be sad. So what? So nothing. That's life. Don't look at it and it will go away."

If one *word* would have been different, just one word; if her tone didn't match the tone I *saw* hours before, I might not have guessed. If the story were less horrific, I might not have known. If she hadn't said "gave *me*" the finger spelling card; if her name hadn't started with "S-y-l..." But in this conversation, I knew. And from Diana's silence on the other end of the line, I knew she knew that I knew. My knees were shaking from fear I couldn't explain…that strange kind of fear arises when you don't know if you could be in danger.

Now everything made sense… paradoxically unbelievable sense. I felt a surgical matter-of-fact-ness and resolve as I spoke now.

"What do I need to do?" I asked.

"She needs to learn how to take the bus. Dr. Holland has never met Sylvia. She *needs* to meet *Sylvia*."

"I understand."   With hands still shaking, I hung up the phone.

Poetry

Two Poems by J.A. Camrose

When the bottom of
that gray hair turns back to its
natural color

-hope

Tonight lying together in bed
I listen to the mesmerizing crisp purring
of autumn leaves in the wind

and ravens
flocking in the night trees
making their
calls

but what warms me the most
is you sleeping inside my arm
and hearing the sound of your breath
while feeling it upon my wrist

-nightlife

Film Review

Three for Your Consideration
Hadley Hury, Film Review Editor

CAROL

Much has been written about director Todd Haynes' affinity for films of the 1950s—and particularly about his affinity for that decade's most emblematic filmmaker of florid melodramas, Douglas Sirk (*Magnificent Obsession, All That Heaven Allows, Written On The Wind, Imitation of Life*). Haynes himself, in frequent interviews, has discussed at length his passionate regard for Sirk, and in 2002 he directed Julianne Moore in *Far from Heaven*, which was a loose adaptation of Sirk's *All That Heaven Allows* (with Jane Wyman and Rock Hudson).

Haynes is not alone in his admiration of these lush, gutsy soaps: most knowledgeable film buffs and a solid majority of critics relish their cinematic energy and prescient probings of the era's social hypocrisies. He also demonstrated his rapt tropism toward period pieces with his take on the world of 1970s glam-rock (*The Velvet Goldmine*, 1998) and in his fine direction of HBO's five-part miniseries remake of *Mildred Pierce*, with Kate Winslet, in 2011. With *Carol*, his new '50s homage featuring Cate Blanchett and Rooney Mara, Haynes may have gone about as far as he can go with his Sirkian obsession.

Adapted by Phyllis Nagy from Patricia Highsmith's 1952 novel  *The Price of Salt*, the film is set in 1952-53 and tells the story of two women who fall in love with one another against a scrupulously evoked backdrop of pop hits by Eddie Fisher, Billie Holiday, and Jo Stafford, ladies having tea at The Ritz in hats and gloves, svelte Packards nosing through midtown Manhattan traffic, and news of Ike's first election airing on small television screens. Judy Becker's production design and Jesse Rosenthal's art direction give *Carol* an appropriate glossiness, and

70

Edward Lachman—who was Haynes' cinematographer on both *Far From Heaven* and *Mildred Pierce*—once again serves with deliberate adoration as acolyte to Haynes' vision. The team's entire mise-en-scene—the use of proscenium-like framing, faces seen through rain-dropped windows, the saturated color palette of aquas, coral, olive, and rich browns shading into chiaroscuro—is so expert in its meta-evocation of the era's cinema that some viewers may actually feel that they are watching a 1950s film within a 1950s film.

The film's greatest attribute is its seamless pictorial authenticity. Its problem is that it has a curiously sluggish and airless quality and only infrequently comes to full-bodied life.

Blanchett plays the title character, a well-to-do Connecticut woman who is divorcing her husband of 10 years and grappling with him over the custody of their young daughter. She meets Terese (Mara) a department store clerk and budding photographer and—tentatively at first and in the face of fiercely prevailing social mores—they embark on a relationship. (With early awards-season buzz, and the film-opening clout of the great Blanchett, the cast and creative team are wisely adhering to the social-issue line in interviews but, sadly, even on that front *Carol* fails to satisfy. The love story-against-societal-odds that should propel the narrative and draw the viewer into the women's sense of discovery is lost in the self-conscious period correctness.) Ironically, *Carol* suffers from Haynes' and his team's hyper-attentiveness to visual detail. Every peripheral action, physical setting, costume design (perfect, by Sandy Powell), every appliance, canned good, radio dial, cigarette lighter, and watch face receives the same lingering, reverential gaze, and is given equal value to the dramatic development—and too often that creates a sense of narrative inertia and, even for such fine actors, a diminution of opportunities for characterization. As usual Blanchett is glamorous and more than capable of holding our attention with her watchful, inward stillness, and Mara countervails with an alert earnestness. Carol's and Terese's exploration, however, feels rather stifled—and it has less to do with our being able to feel the social strictures that confound them and more to do with the director's heavy indications and prescriptive style. A certain muted delicacy might be argued as appropriate for both the era and the material, but when the care and mastery in evoking a period outweighs the drama, our appreciation is left too frequently to dwell on contextual detail rather than the human focus.

Haynes has an acute sense of texture and tone, but since he has so frequently drawn comparisons with his and Sirk's films it's difficult for us not to do the same. The dire trials of the female protagonists in Sirk's melodramas may be nearly over-the-top, but they are full-blooded sagas that viewers can sink their teeth into. Even more, their narrative insistence and Technicolor vibrancy sink their teeth into the viewer—and don't let go. His movies have a subversive power, seething up like lava beneath the suppressive order of '50s society and bursting from the screen. Even with their sometimes overripe high-voltage garishness (which consigned them largely to the camp category for 20-30 years) Sirk's melodramas are undeniably watchable. *Carol* lacks this emotional immediacy: though Blanchett and Mara have a few subtly moving scenes, much of the film remains flat, static, and distant. A few ravishing images may resonate, but the viewer too often is stranded at a remove.

Haynes is an intelligent filmmaker. His passionate regard for film history as well as for source material and craft are more worthy than much of the sophomoric slapdash that unmemorably fills cineplex screens. We can have every reason to hope that, now fifty-five, he may yet make a more robust and invigorating film, one proving that even his Mannerist art can give us more than a pastiche of painstakingly curated images and take on—as Douglas Sirk himself might have titled a piece—a life of its own.

TRUMBO

Trumbo is an important film because it succeeds in both educating and entertaining. It throws into sharp relief and lends urgent voice to issues in our socio-political landscape today. Set primarily between 1947 and 1960 the film focuses on the Hollywood blacklist and its ramifications for one of filmdom's most adroit screenwriters. It examines, through a film industry lens, the toxic Red Menace hysteria brewed during the

dark and disgraceful days of the House Un-American Activities Committee. In 21st-Century politics, increasingly degraded by right-wing politicians and media outlets using fear and bullying in their strategy to divide and conquer at any cost, the cautionary tale of *Trumbo* has a reeking freshness.

Bryan Cranston, multiple Emmy Award winner for "Breaking Bad", is superb as Dalton Trumbo, whose scripts for box-office hits like *A Guy Named Joe* and *Kitty Foyle*—and later works as diverse as *Spartacus, The Fixer,* and *Papillon*—placed him in the upper ranks of Hollywood wordsmiths. Like many American artists, intellectuals, and labor leaders, Trumbo became a Communist during the days of Fascism's ascendancy between the World Wars. Once World War II ended and the Cold War began in earnest, Trumbo and other "sympathizers" were soon targeted by the HUAC. In the perversion of constitutional rights and our body politic that ensued—and which most heinously came to be personified by Sen. Joe McCarthy—even some liberal Democrats like Edward G. Robinson (played convincingly here by Michael Stuhlbarg) are thrown to the zealous demagogues. Some, including Trumbo, are jailed, others crack and willingly give names, and many lose their careers, their families, and a few even their lives. But Trumbo fights to survive, writing scripts pseudonymously. The necessary deception ironically garners him two Academy Awards (for *Roman Holiday* and *The Brave One*), neither of which he could claim.

Jay Roach's direction, though lacking in verve and cinematic imagination, is respectfully thoughtful. Its deliberateness succeeds in making the story's most salient points clear, and for an important story that is an asset that needs no apology. Occasional lapses of energy seem more attributable to John McNamara's workmanlike adaptation of Bruce Cook's 1977 book *Dalton Trumbo*. That said, *Trumbo* never succumbs to the belabored pomposity of some bio-pics. It has an integrity and inner logic of construction and pace—and some vivid supporting performances—that keep it both watchable and engrossing.

Helen Mirren as Hollywood columnist Hedda Hopper is wonderful. It's another of the film's assets that many viewers will learn for the first time that Hopper was not merely the sometimes cleverly bitchy troublemaker with the signature hats or, more latterly, a talk-show guest regular who sought to disarm with a feigned scattiness. She held a very influential bully pulpit and, most treacherously in this era,

73

was a vicious red-baiter who wrecked careers and lives. Rather than go for broke, Mirren uses her scenes judiciously to limn this harridan's bitter, hard-won, calculating knowledge of Hollywood values, her steely, monomaniacal determination for revenge, and the cold, rather exhausted amorality from which to distract she employed the colorful chapeaux, fluty grande-dame voice, and straight-razor smiles. It is a brilliantly considered performance and Mirren executes it with surgical incisiveness.

Cranston's performance is quietly riveting: his portrayal of Trumbo's tenacity in adhering to principles never grandstands—it's pragmatic and worldly-wise—and he evinces the writer's felicity of language and dry wit more as survival techniques than as a flaunting of epigrams. Diane Lane, as his strong and steadfast wife Cleo, has an almost impassive solidity that works well here. The role gives her little to do but she manages to evoke an essence of bemused patience and common sense that, by all historical accounts, were essential to her own survival as well as that of her husband and family. And the careful progress of the film is enlivened by the hijinks of John Goodman as a low-rent producer for whom Trumbo grinds out schlock during the direst days of his blacklisting, and the canny cameos of Stuhlbarg as Robinson and Dean O'Gorman as Kirk Douglas.

SPOTLIGHT

Spotlight is a solid piece of good old-fashioned moviemaking, and it proves that there can be some aspects of old-fashioned moviemaking that need no apology. Almost austere in its refusal to wow audiences with cinematic bells, whistles, and flourishes, it earns its suspense through the carefully calibrated teamwork of a fine ensemble of actors and an uncluttered focus, and is a potent reminder that investigative journalism can be capable of eschewing the self-regard and sensationalism it is often heir to and can even at times attain a significant level of moral gravity.

Early in the film, which is set in Boston largely in 2001, the central conflict is established in a conversation between Cardinal Bernard Law and the new editor at The Boston Globe, Martin Baron (recently arrived from Miami). "The city flourishes when its great institutions work together," says the cardinal to the newspaper editor during a get-acquainted chat in the rectory. Len Cariou plays the Cardinal with the expansive bonhomie of a man used to having his way, and we detect that he must artfully conceal his surprise when the editor—Liev Schreiber in an elegantly restrained performance—demurs from this cozy vision of civic harmony and politely but firmly posits that the paper must stand alone.

A small group of reporters at The Globe then spends several months digging into the Boston archdiocese's role in covering up the sexual abuse of dozens of children by priests. It's a somber but engaging investigation, and it is testament to the success of the film's tone and pace that director Tom McCarthy and his co-screenwriter Josh Singer are able to infuse office work such as keyboarding, examining old files and records, and answering telephones, with emotion, suspense, and narrative verve. Based closely on actual events, *Spotlight*—which takes its name from the Globe's investigative team, headed by Robby Robinson (Michael Keaton in an intelligently lean, crisply delineated performance)—becomes a riveting detective story, a realistic newsroom drama, and a finely detailed procedural focusing on both the human particulars of institutional immorality and the seismic socio-political ramifications of the scandal and its uncovering.

Raised in the largely Roman Catholic establishment of Boston, Robby is an old acquaintance of an unctuous p-r man for the church (Paul Guilfoyle) and plays golf with an attorney who handled some of the archdiocese's unsavory business (James Sheridan). The reporters working with Robby—Mike Rezendes (Mark Ruffalo), Sacha Pfeiffer (Rachel McAdams), and Matt Carroll (Brian d'Arcy James)—also come from Catholic backgrounds, and have their own conflicted feelings about the investigation. The actors' self-effacement and delicate sense of partnering lend a sense of lived-in dailiness and believability to their work as the Spotlight team. There's never the least hint of grandstanding in any of the performances, yet each character is distinct, subtly evinced, true—and the cast is further enhanced by expert work from Stanley Tucci (as the pragmatically worldly-wise but deeply humane attorney for some of the abuse survivors), Billy Crudup, and John Slattery.

Critic Richard Brody, writing in newyorker.com (November 10, 2015) voices what seems the most legitimate potential dissent from the general acclamation *Spotlight* has received. Brody insists that by adhering solely to the newsroom team and its exacting procedures for breaking an accurate and complete story the film misses the opportunity to look more deeply into the personal stories of the survivors of abuse, the psychology of priests who perpetrated it, and the deep-rooted systemic corruption of the hierarchy that refused to deal with it—including not only the higher church officials who covered it up but their complicit attorneys as well as other civic leaders who turned blind eyes. There is one brief scene in which one of the team questions a former priest at the door of his house about his fondling of children. With wide-eyed ingenuousness the man declares that, yes, he did that, but that he "derived no pleasure from it himself". It's stunningly clear that in his mind, ergo, no real crime occurred. The kind of long-bred institutional sophistry, self-protection, and arrogance that can breed this degree of delusion would certainly make for an interesting film, but in two hours even an intelligently ambitious film cannot do everything. One can understand precisely what Brody means when he says that *Spotlight* left him wanting more—but that is because there is so much more to examine, not because McCarthy and Singer did not handle well the manageable focus they chose.

Indeed, *Spotlight* is defined and succeeds as much by what it chooses to leave out as by what it includes. Journalists in film are often portrayed as crusading idealists or amoral, egocentric leeches. Here we see them as human beings who, without succumbing to either a sense of self-aggrandizement or wary cynicism, do the job of trying to confront evil—as a team of conscientious professionals who take on the dangerous hydra of an entrenched system of power operating without accountability.

Poetry

One for Addie by Will Walton

One for Addie

I slide my hand inside the glove,
squeeze it a few times, then bring it to my nose.
What once smelled like oiled leather & sweat,
now reeks of stale smoke & permanence.
What once reminded me of my childhood—
years spent crouched behind a batter,
begging the runner on first--
now prompts an image
of me dusting the ash from my stiff, void cat,
& lowering her into a trash bag.
This old mitt was just luckier—
it was packed away in a metal trunk,
in the farthest corner of the house.
She was behind the refrigerator, alone,
trying only to stay cool while her body burned
& carbon monoxide filled her sweet lungs.

Short Story

Moral Imperative
By C.W. Spooner

Have I got a story for you! You probably won't believe it but I swear it's all true. It's about two friends of mine, Adrian and Angela, a couple in their late twenties, and I'll bet it is the strangest story you've heard in a while. My name is Wilson—everybody calls me Will—and Adrian and I go back a long way, back to our grammar school days. Basically he's a good guy. His concept of right and wrong gets skewed every now and then, but doesn't everybody's? I mean under pressure, extreme pressure, all of us will bend a little. Am I wrong?

But … I digress. Let me tell you the story and you can decide.

Adrian and Angela moved in together about a year ago. That is to say Adrian moved into Angela's apartment, a nice two-bedroom unit in a decent neighborhood. Angela mentioned the possibility one night in an intimate moment, if you know what I mean, and Adrian jumped at the offer, said yes so fast the poor girl didn't have time to change her mind. You see, Adrian was up to his eyeballs in student loans, couldn't afford the payments, and saw himself going down the drain. Angela had her own student loans to deal with, but at least she had a job. She's a registered nurse working at a local hospital.

Adrian's career choice was to go to film school at USC. He wants to be the next Steven Spielberg and make blockbuster movies, but the best he could find coming out of school was a gig with an outfit that makes industrial training films. Hey, it's experience, right? So he takes the job on a contract and works for the company as an assistant director for about a year. And then—nothing. He's out of work. His bank account is draining rapidly. He's a few weeks from being flat broke. But then Angela threw him that lifeline, cut his expenses in half (or less) and kept a roof over his head. So he moved in and settled into the grind of trying to find work, trying to keep Angela happy, trying to keep his head above water.

You get the picture.

Angela is a sweet, sweet girl. Cute. Intelligent. Hard-working. And—here's the kicker—she loves to dance. I guess it's a way to decompress after a long week at the hospital, but Angela loves to go out to a hot club and dance her buns off. This is not Adrian's thing, but he goes along with it, mainly because after a couple of drinks and a night on the dance floor, Angela becomes a love-making tigress. Her passion knows no bounds. So Adrian dances till his feet ache and his ankles swell, with one eye on the clock. "Honey, think it's time to go? Maybe we should call it a night?"

Know what I mean?

So, one Saturday night they are in line outside this mega-popular club, waiting to get in. Angela is dressed to the nines in a clingy little dress that shows a lot of leg, and take my word for it, they are nice legs, especially when she slips on her Jimmy Choo knock-offs. How she can dance in those heels I'll never know. She must be related to Tina Turner.

But again … I digress.

Adrian is doing his best to keep up, wearing his Ralph Lauren jeans and a white linen shirt, untucked of course, unbuttoned at the collar, the sleeves rolled up a couple of turns. Off in the distance they can see the fireworks at Disneyland lighting up the night sky, the muffled boom boom boom arriving on a three-second delay.

The crowd waiting to get in is stretched out around the block. The security guys keep saying it will be a forty-minute wait. A few people leave the club and few go in, but security sticks with the forty minute story. After a while, Angela has to pee. She holds it as long as she can but finally decides to head across the street to a service station with a food mart and use the bathroom. First she buys a couple of packs of gum to establish herself as a paying customer, then she waits in a short line for the ladies room. She is on her way back across the street when she sees Adrian heading toward her in a big hurry. She can see police cars converging at the front of the club, their lights flashing, cops climbing out, wading into the crowd.

"There was a fight," Adrian says. "Some girl got stomped. Come on, let's get out of here."

On the way home, he tells Angela what he saw. Some people coming out of the club bumped into a girl waiting to go in. The girl yelled *WTF* or some such and before he knew what was happening,

79

fists were flying, hair was being pulled, guys were jumping in to defend their women, and it was a full-blown brawl. The girl who got bumped wound up on the ground and she wasn't moving. At that point, Adrian decided to get out of there.

And that's the way the night ended. No dancing for Angela. No hot sex for Adrian. An all-around disappointing evening. Except for the part of the story Adrian wasn't telling.

***

The next morning Adrian was up early and out of the apartment. He left a note for Angela saying he had to meet a guy about a possible job. He picked up the newspaper from the stoop on the way out and beat it down to his local Coffee Bean. He could not wait to check his iPhone and see the video he shot outside the club. And when he watched it all he could say was "Oh my God oh my God" oh my God, over and over. He captured nearly all of the fight, including the girl throwing the first punch, including the ones who took turns stomping her head while she was down on the pavement, their faces clearly visible.

That's right: "Oh my God!"

He sat back in his chair and closed his eyes for a minute. Then he remembered the newspaper. He opened it and immediately saw the headline story about the incident at the club. The girl who was bumped, who took a swing at the woman who bumped her, who wound up down on the pavement getting stomped, was dead. They rushed her to the nearest trauma center but she never regained consciousness.

Adrian grabbed his phone and watched the video several more times. He picked up the paper and saw a companion column to the headline story written by a well-known columnist—let's call him Scoop Smith—decrying the fact that nobody came to the aid of the girl as she was on the ground being kicked, how in spite of several people pulling out their camera phones to film the fight, no one wanted to come forward and help the police investigation.

There was a payphone just outside the coffee shop. Before Adrian headed for home, he called the switchboard at the newspaper and was transferred to Scoop Smith's extension. He left a voice message saying that he had important information about the club incident and that he would call again on Monday morning to discuss it. Adrian headed back to the apartment, hoping he could contain himself and actually wait until Monday.

***

I know Angela pretty well and she is the epitome of a solid citizen, a straight shooter, the kind of person you want to be a nurse—your nurse. Sunday evening she curled up on the couch with Adrian to watch the news. The lead story was about the fight outside the club and the death of the young woman. Her name was Lia Nguyen. She was a recent graduate of a local college, a part-time model, and she wrote poetry as a hobby. On the TV screen flashed a still photo taken by someone in the crowd that showed the fight in progress, a girl with long brown hair on the ground, the group around her in obvious combat posture. At the edge of the crowd was a guy in a white shirt, crouched down to get a better view, with his camera phone held out in front of him.

Angela grabbed the remote and hit the pause button. "Oh my God, Adrian! Is that you? In the white shirt? That is you! What are you doing? You were standing there filming the whole thing? You didn't try to help her?"

Adrian did his best to deflect, but he could see that it was a lost cause. It was him and there was no way to deny it. He tried to explain that the guys in the fight were built like NFL linemen; at five nine and a buck seventy-five, there was no way he could help the girl. It wasn't long before Angela was demanding to see the video. He did some more foot dragging but finally got his phone and played it for her.

"You have to take this to the police. This is evidence. You can't just sit here. A girl is dead…" Angela let him have it with both barrels. She was disgusted to be sitting with him knowing now what he had done.

Adrian took a deep breath and made his case as forcefully as possible. "Look, Angela, this video is worth big money to these media whores. They pay for information like this. Look at the student loans you and I are struggling with. We could get enough from this to make a huge dent in that debt, if not pay it off altogether. We'd be stupid to just turn this over to the cops. Stupid!"

Adrian told me the debate raged on for more than an hour, loaded with tears and accusations, plus a discussion of morals and ethics in a morally and ethically ambiguous world. In the end, there was no way for Angela to be swayed. She issued an ultimatum: either he would turn the video over to the police or she would call them herself and turn him in. She agreed, after much pleading on Adrian's part, that he would do this by the time she came home from work on Monday.

Knowing Angela, I will never understand how Adrian bargained for that much time.

***

I can tell you that Adrian is a hard-charger when he sets his mind to it. He was at it early Monday morning, as soon as Angela left for work. The first thing he did was to upload the video to a bootleg copy of editing software on his iPad, a powerful package that he'd copied from the servers at the industrial film company where he worked. The video was even more striking on his iPad screen. He could zoom and edit and frame the content and generally enhance the impact of what he had captured. He couldn't wait to show the results to Scoop Smith.

He found a payphone on the corner near a newsstand and called the newspaper. They patched him through to Smith's desk. Adrian made it short and to the point: he had clear footage of the attack on Lia Nguyen, footage that showed the faces of the people who stomped her do death. He wanted $120,000 for exclusive rights. Smith laughed and hemmed and hawed, but the bottom line was that he would have to see the video in order to determine if it was worth the asking price. They agreed to meet at a Starbucks in Towne Center. Adrian cautioned Smith to come alone; if there was any hint that he brought along a crew, or the police, the meeting would never happen.

***

My friend Adrian is a clever guy, but he is no James Bond. He thought of a hundred ways that Scoop Smith could trip him up—bring a crew with telephoto lenses, alert the cops, wear a wire, and on and on. He decided to go through with the meeting anyway and showed up at

82

the Starbucks forty minutes early. He plugged in his iPad and sat nursing a grande latte just like a half dozen other guys. At one point, he saw a discarded newspaper on a nearby table; on the front page was another article under Scoop Smith's byline. It seems that Lia lived in a neighborhood populated by senior citizens. She was friendly and chatty with them and did little favors for them from time to time. Her neighbors loved her and were grieving her loss.

Right about then, Smith walked through the door. Adrian recognized him from his picture in the newspaper. After he ordered a tall Pike Place and found a seat, Adrian let him sit there for ten minutes while he scanned the area to make sure he came alone and wasn't communicating with anyone. Finally he picked up his iPad and approached Smith's table.

The introductions were brief. Adrian played the video footage a couple of times and Smith was duly impressed. Adrian had the goods, just as advertised. Then the two of them went into negotiation mode. Smith said, "look, kid, we don't normally pay for information. Know what I mean? Checkbook journalism? We have our standards. Your video is impressive but I doubt that I can get that kind of money out of my editors. Besides, we're print media and you're peddling video."

Adrian was prepared for this and he held firm. "Take it or leave it. Your parent company has TV stations, and there are a dozen other media outlets that I can reach out to. I thought of you first because of the column you wrote about the girl. I think a Pulitzer would look nice on your mantle, don't you?"

In the end, Smith agreed to take the deal back to his editors. Journalistic ethics be damned. Adrian would call him later that afternoon. And that was it. They went their separate ways. Adrian took a roundabout route back to the apartment, afraid he was being followed.

***

He may not be James Bond, but my pal Adrian is nobody's fool. Back at the apartment, he plugged external drives into his iPad and made a couple of copies of his video. He had a bulletproof idea for a place to hide the copies, just in case.

Angela called during her lunch break to see if Adrian had contacted the police. When he tried to sidestep and back-peddle, she hung up on him. In his mind he still had a few hours to make a deal with Smith; they had agreed that he would call at around 3:00pm. Adrian left the apartment and drove around looking for another payphone. It turns out they are not that easy to find, but he finally located one in the parking lot of a convenience store. The call to Scoop Smith did not go well.

"Look, kid, my editors won't go for it. At least not for the one-twenty large. I could maybe get you a few thousand, but that's about it. You know this is evidence in a murder investigation. You are looking at obstruction of justice or some shit like that. Your best bet is to call the police, give 'em what you've got."

So Adrian told him where he could stick his few thousand and hung up the phone. When he got back to the apartment, Angela had been there ahead of him. His suitcase and several trash bags stuffed with his things were sitting near the front door with a note.

"Do not be here when I get home. Leave the key in the mailbox. I cannot be with a man who has no concept of morality."

Just like that it was over. Adrian went to the fridge and pulled out a beer. There were a few cold ones left and he decided to drink them all before he left. He would miss Angela, but hey, a guy's gotta do what a guy's gotta do. If she didn't want in on his debt reduction plan, that just meant more for him.

***

Good old Adrian. Morally compromised, ethically challenged, whatever you want to call him. Even after three beers, my old pal still had the ability to think on his feet. He was about to head to the kitchen for another beer when he heard car doors slam out on the street. He went to the window and saw two guys standing next to a gray Ford sedan, one of them checking his phone, the other leafing through a notepad. Dark rumpled suits, soft-soled shoes, aviator shades— obviously cops. How did they find him? Was it Angela? Scoop Smith? Or just good police work? To this day he doesn't know the answer.

Adrian immediately whipped out his cell phone and dialed 9-1-1. He hurried through the preliminaries with the dispatcher, even as the cops were walking up to the front door, and told the woman on the phone that he had just realized he had video footage of the fatal beating that took place Saturday night. He needed to speak to the police as soon as possible. She pointedly explained that this was *not* an emergency and that he should call the police directly. Adrian pretended that the connection was bad and hung up. When he answered the knock on the door and the detectives flashed their badges, he was ready.

"Boy that was quick. I just got off the phone with 9-1-1. Come on in, I have something to show you."

***

So, that's how Adrian came to live with me. Angela won't have anything to do with him, won't even consider taking him back; she's found someone else to take her dancing. Adrian sleeps on my couch and he's not bad as roommates go, picks up after himself, cleans up his own mess, and rinses out the sink after he shaves. In the meantime, he is hard at work on a screenplay. He is sure it can be a major motion picture, one of those based-on-a-true-story sensations. His concept is to eventually cut the real-life video footage into the film to give it that undeniable stamp of reality. The police have never figured out that he has copies hidden away, though they had their doubts about his story. The district attorney hasn't charged him with obstruction, so far. After all, he has that 9-1-1 call going for him.

We've had some long talks about what he's doing and whether it is right or wrong. Of course, Adrian relates everything to a movie. In this case it's Clint Eastwood's *Unforgiven*, the scene at the end where William Munny blasts the saloon owner with a shotgun and Little Bill Dagget says, "You, sir, are a cowardly son of a bitch. You just shot an unarmed man." Munny says, "Well he should have armed himself..."

I asked Adrian to expand on that thought. Here he is in his own words:

"Will, my friend, let's face it. We live in a world where Wall Street CEO's can preside over a near-global meltdown of the financial system, throw our economy into deep recession, cause millions of people to lose their jobs, their homes, and their life savings. And what are the consequences? Those executives see their firms bailed out by the taxpayers because they are too big to fail. Then they pay themselves and their minions bonuses in the millions of dollars, and collectively spend hundreds of millions more to make sure that tough regulations are not voted into law. Lives are ruined, completely destroyed, and do any of these CEO's face prosecution or do jail time? Not a one. And what about students like me who took the easy money thrown at us by the banks—at eight percent interest or more? Now that interest rates are cut in half, can we refinance our loans and reduce the soul-sucking payments? Hell no! And why? Because those same Wall Street CEO's spend hundreds of millions to make sure legislation to help students never comes to a vote in Congress. Yes, Lia Nguyen is dead. But there is nothing I can do to bring her back. So, why shouldn't I capitalize on the video I shot? Why shouldn't I pay off my student loans with 'fuck you money'? Why just stand there and take the shotgun blast in the gut? No my dear, naïve Will, I choose to fight back."

All I can say to that is *Wow!* Adrian could rationalize a heart attack. You probably noticed that last quote about *fuck you money* is also from a movie: Matt Damon's character in *Promised Land*. With Adrian, it's all about movies.

Now here is the punchline: there is a production company that wants to make Adrian's film. They are negotiating for an option on the screenplay and they're currently offering him $50,000. Not bad for openers. And let me tell you something: I've read the screenplay and it is damn good.

My friend Adrian has armed himself.

Poetry

George and his Wife by John Horvath Jr.

George And His Wife Lay On The Beach

You and I, George, are characters
Who lack a novel and a novelist.
We've neither form nor sense except
another makes it from our words.

You mean your diary, I suspect.

I mean a grand and vacant something
So MORE than what we might say or do
(We really haven't freedom to do much
but lay on this beach and wait, forever
watching the circling birds,
the arc of waves upon the beach.)

God's book of life you mean--
the right and wrong of us.
(But to himself: more likely
the legend of St George
and his slain dragon bitch
who thinks too much; cerebral
women are such a pain).

No. We are being watched.
I sense the reader of these words
who makes us live our lives
repeatedly and without change.
This same sun, this ever beach,
those motionless gulls above.

They're pelicans.
You, there! Reader!
How dare you!
Relax. I've chased them off.

Poetry

Emily's Eyes by Allen Frederick Stein

Emily's Eyes
(for E.D.)

Look closely at the picture,
the only one authenticated
as the genuine Emily.
See how the eyes don't align
conventionally, properly.
Each turns from the other,
avoiding binocular resolution.

The name assigned for this
is Exotropic Strabismus,
commonly called Wall Eye.
Each eye is on its own
as it looks sidewise,
away from what is directly before it.

The medical texts tell us
misaligned eyes send separate images.
A child's brain ignores these mixed messages,
resolves them readily into one,
but the adult's may develop Diplopia,
or double vision.
In Emily's case this is extreme.
She may have wished it so—
recall that she told an uncomprehending friend
that she loved to "buffet the sea,"
loved the danger—
this from a woman who'd never boarded ship,
never felt heavy wave
smack against straining planks.

But no danger could have been dearer to her
than that of sailing a true course
in diverging directions
toward a single destination
never to be reached.

Thus, Emily's left eye,
which peers far over your right shoulder,
even as her slightly broad nose
points straight at you,
may be spying that certain slant of light,
the one that weighs so heavy, winter afternoons
(note the downward turn of the lip on that side),
while the right may see,
well past your left shoulder,
a bobolink chirping praise on high
under an orchard's leafy dome
(hence the upward tilt of the lip's right corner?).
The possibilities are many—
the housefly and the hummingbird,
the frost and the flower,
a smile easy as a star and death's stiff stare,
the choiring meeting house,
the silent alabaster chamber.

She wrote that the brain is wider than the sky.
Hers, at any rate, was capacious enough
to hold till the end
a bifurcated vision.
She gave no poem a title,
for she knew no true journey was ever finished,
knew all was ever in tenuous balance,
endless tension.

 "Strabismus" is from the Greek for "squinting,"
and though Emily in the photo is wide-eyed,
she peered hard always,
toward something impinging and inevitable

90

on the very periphery of sight,
far beyond whatever tokens, sinister or sublime,
might be visible at any given moment
to either searching eye.

She knew it was, at last, a wall
that she eyed, and had from the first,
and that, unreachable,
it circumscribed all, enclosed all.
Beyond it, perhaps,
resided an encompassing resolution,
then again, perhaps not.
But still she sailed her double course toward it.

Look more closely now at Emily.
Draw your face, your eyes, close to her own.
Notice, when you're close enough,
that she becomes twin Emilys,
but not quite identical,
one certain that faith is indeed a fine brave thing,
the other no less certain it's an invention,
timid and expedient.
Both Emilys hint at a crooked smile,
as if neither is ever unaware
that the other might be right, after all,
—but only might be.

Pull back a bit now.
Watch the two resolve into Emily,
buffeting the waves,
toward the unattainable wall
that is never beyond her vision.

Poetry

No Early Birds by Elizabeth Crowell

No Early Birds

At the wooden doors
of this New England church,
its needle-steeple upward in a field of maples,
a sign is posted to warn those
who want to rummage through the goods too soon.
Perhaps arriving in advance
will get me a place before the rest,
a route down the church basement hall
to the acre of tables, set with
bone china cups, cameo pins, and Mason Jars,
but when I think of starting out again
in hopes of what I do not even know yet,
I remember how my son tried this,
coming so soon into the vast worldliness
that he never drew a breath.

And so here I am outside
where white fields of spring blossoms
against a stone wall thicken like deserted linens
and if you ask me what grief is,
its that short, cordoned rope,
the strict hours of life to death
that I see across each of us,
these desperate souls on the sidewalk
pushing towards
the hope of an object found
on the shaky slope of a folded table.
I scan the muddied, spring ground,
kicking my sneakers in a skyless motion,
and eye the spring worms floundering, unfound

with my son beside me
in the dark coat of what it takes to die so young,

Commentary

Noel Mawer Short Story Award Contest

For the first time in its seven year history, *Lost Coast Review* will be sponsoring a writing award contest. Noel Mawer is the long-time Book Review Editor of *Lost Coast Review*. She is retiring in 2016 and in her honor, we are inaugurating an annual award for short story writing. The *Noel Mawer Short Story Award* will be awarded to the best story of 4000 words or less received by June15, 2016. The winner will receive a $100 cash prize and the award winning short story will be published in the Summer, 2016 issue of *Lost Coast Review* and be eligible for a *Pushcart Prize* nomination from *Lost Coast Review* for works published during 2016.

An entry fee of $10 will be charged for each entry in the contest. A writer may enter as many times as he or she wishes.

The deadline for submissions is June 15, 2016.

To enter go to the contest page at http://avignonpress.com/contests/

Look for the announcement of our annual **Poetry Award Contest** and **Essay Award Contest** in future issues of *Lost Coast Review* and at http://www.lostcoastreview.com .

Submissions

Submission Guidelines – Short Stories, Poetry, Reviews, etc.

Lost Coast Review welcomes unsolicited submissions of short stories, poetry, book reviews, film reviews, photography or art (Must be black and white to appear in the paperback version of *Lost Coast Review*. Color art may appear in the online version only.) Commentary on artistic and sociopolitical topics is also occasionally accepted, if it is of superior merit. *Lost Coast Review* does not pay authors for their work.

Guidelines:

1. It may take a while to get back to you. So please be patient.

2. Submissions by email only. Include a brief description of your work in the body of the email, including the category (short story, poem, book review, film review, commentary, art or photography). Attach the work itself as a Word document (.doc or .docx) or, if art, as a jpeg. Note: To submit a short story to the Noel Mawer Short Story Award Contest, please follow the directions at:
http://avignonpress.com/contests/

3. We normally limit poetry to no more than three poems per issue by a single poet and short stories to 4,000 words or less.

4. Please include your name, contact information, and previous publishing history or any kind of credits that could be interesting to readers. Include these at the end of your submission.

5. If your piece is accepted, we will proofread and edit it. If anything further than that is necessary, we will first run changes by you for your final approval.

6. By submitting an item, you grant us your consent to publish it in *Lost Coast Review*. The *Review* asks only for the right to publish a story or poem for the first time, on the Web and in print. All rights revert to the author after publication by *Lost Coast Review*. All accepted work will be archived on the *Lost Coast Review* website.

7. If you want to submit your material elsewhere in the meantime, that's fine. Just be sure to let us know if it gets published somewhere else before we've had a chance to respond.

8. You may withdraw your submission prior to publication by contacting us and identifying the item by title and author.

9. By submitting material, you are acknowledging that you solely own the copyright and agree to the above guidelines.

10. Use the email address below to submit work and label it *submission*.

Contact Us: Our email address is: info@avignonpress.com